CLASSICAL ARCHAEOLOGY
IN THE FIELD: APPROACHES

Current and forthcoming titles in the Classical World Series

Classical World Series

CLASSICAL ARCHAEOLOGY IN THE FIELD: APPROACHES

**Laurence Bowkett, Stephen Hill,
Diana & K.A. Wardle**

Bristol Classical Press

General Editor: John H. Betts
Series Editor: Michael Gunningham

Cover illustration: a sixth-century BC clay plaque
from Pente Skouphia near Corinth.

First published in 2001 by
Bristol Classical Press
an imprint of
Gerald Duckworth & Co. Ltd
61 Frith Street
London W1D 3JL
e-mail: inquiries@duckworth-publishers.co.uk
Website: www.ducknet.co.uk

A catalogue record for this book is available
from the British Library

ISBN 1-85399-617-3

Printed in Great Britain by
Antony Rowe Ltd

Contents

List of Illustrations

Acknowledgements

We are very grateful to Gina Coulthard of the British Insitute at Ankara for writing the section on applications and funding; to Roger White, Sally Exon and other colleagues in the Birmingham University Field Archaeology Unit for assistance with copies of photographs, plans and diagrams; and to Graham Norrie who has prepared many of the necessary photographs.

Chapter 1
Introduction

Almost everyone who has explored the Classical World, whether through reading the literature of the Greeks and Romans, visiting the monuments they created or searching the virtual realm of Internet sites, feels an increasing wonder and excitement about the lives of our distant ancestors or the achievements which are fundamental to the development of European culture and civilisation. Part of that excitement arises from the recognition that this is another of the frontiers of human knowledge where new discoveries are made almost every year, discoveries which can fundamentally alter our understanding of Classical civilisation. Many of these result from systematic fieldwork – recording, survey and excavation. Others arise from the study of the finds made and the interpretative processes that help to turn raw data into historical reconstruction.

This book sets out the principles and methods which underpin the ways in which, today, research in Classical archaeology in the field is rapidly expanding. As practising archaeologists, we have not attempted to produce an encyclopaedia documenting the results of decades and centuries of work in the countries which comprise what was once the Classical world. Rather, we have aimed to explain how the work of discovery proceeds and how the new information acquired is interpreted. We hope to enable readers to explore for themselves the new discoveries made and reported each year and begin to understand the mosaic of data which enriches understanding of the ancient world.

We plan, in due course, to produce a series of case studies which will enable the application of these methods to be followed through in current projects from planning to publication. Four projects in which we have been involved will feature in these case studies and have been referred to regularly in the present volume: the Late Bronze Age and Iron Age settlement at Assiros in Greek Macedonia, the Roman city of Knossos in Crete, the Roman fort at the Lunt in Coventry and the Early Christian church at Çiftlik on the north coast of Turkey. In the meantime we shall be maintaining, as far as possible, a web site at: http://www.artsweb.bham.ac.uk/aha/classarch.htm which will provide signposts to the wealth of 'sites' – both archaeological and virtual –

which offer suitable material from many different countries for further study. These illustrate the methods of archaeologists as well as their discoveries and demonstrate the expanding contribution they make to understanding the Classical World.

It is important to declare immediately that the term 'Classical archaeology' now has a much broader application than the restricted Victorian interpretation of the expression which included little more than the study of Greek vase-painting, Greek architecture and, perhaps, Roman engineering and military architecture. All these subjects are well served in other books and we shall not revisit them.

'Classical' and 'archaeology' are, of course, both terms which call for definition. Looking at 'archaeology' first – for this is above all a book about archaeology – the word derives from the Greek words *archaios* and *logos* and essentially means study of the past, or study of old things. In practice, archaeology concerns itself with the material remains of the past and, as such, can be distinguished from history, which is traditionally concerned with the study of the written evidence of the past.

Perceptions change almost as fast as fashions and for the past fifty years the divergence of history and archaeology – as disciplines which use different methodologies – has been fostered by the rivalry between scholars on either side of this apparent divide, who have each tried to demonstrate the more objective basis of their own field. In truth, history and archaeology are but the opposite sides of a single coin – on one the legend and on the other an image. Both disciplines seek to discover a greater knowledge of the past and, at last, both sets of scholars are recognising, especially in relation to the Classical world, that archaeology and ancient history complement each other very effectively. Although the two disciplines overlap when there is both archaeological and written evidence from which to draw an account of past events, only archaeology can be used to provide an account of past human activity when there is no written record.

Archaeology has often been described as the 'handmaiden' of history because history can tell us what people thought whilst archaeology can only describe what they did. The term 'handmaiden' is unacceptably gendered at the beginning of the twenty-first century and it implies a subservience to history which few, if any, archaeologists would now accept. Even the idea that only history can tell us about past people's thinking is now challenged since archaeological remains of prehistoric societies can, for instance, be extremely informative about ancient belief systems. Archaeologists are now more likely to take the view that historical evidence, where it is available, is merely one form of evidence which must be taken into account when conducting research and so, far from being the subservient discipline, archaeology actually encompasses a much broader field of knowledge.

Looking at the differences between history and archaeology is actually a very effective way of achieving a definition of the latter. Historians depend on evidence which is written and often refer to contemporary documents as their *primary* source material. But for the archaeologist, such written material is actually a form of *secondary* evidence since it is an account of, or opinion about, events or personalities. Somebody wrote it down and that somebody must have had a purpose for doing so. If the purpose was, for instance, political or nationalistic, then the objectivity of the account must be seriously questioned. More recent historical records, such as censuses, may be relatively objective, but for the periods covered in this book the objectivity of the written accounts should always be considered. The earliest historians, themselves ancient Greeks, were well aware of the problems caused by the kind of evidence available to them. The historian Herodotus, writing his account of the Persian Wars in the fifth century BC, regularly referred to the existence of more than one version of the same event and frequently wrote down both versions without necessarily saying which was the more reliable. In view of this (and also because of his inclusion of digressions such as his long account of Egypt) he has been condemned as being less scientific than his successor Thucydides, who presented his own version of the Peloponnesian War and stuck to it. Yet the approach of Herodotus is actually more honest and his digressions are full of fascinating social and geographical comment which are often of more use – at least to archaeologists – than the more polished observations and deductions of Thucydides, who was, in the last analysis, a disgruntled right-wing general with private means.

When looking at Classical archaeology, it is important to remember that archaeology has an application which goes well beyond the time frame accessible to historians. The methodology of archaeology has had to be developed in the context of societies which had not yet benefited from the invention of writing. The origin of the human species is a subject which is well outside the scope of the present volume but, in order to place the Classical period into a broader context, it is worth noting that there has been human activity around the Mediterranean and in Europe since at least half a million years ago. Even when put together, the Classical, medieval and modern periods do not account for one percent of that vast epoch of time, but archaeology has to take account of human activity through that entire time span.

What ultimately distinguishes archaeology from history, and what therefore defines it, is method. Archaeology as a discipline has much in common with science, and the principles which direct archaeological practice and many of the methods used by archaeologists are scientific. Archaeologists follow the basic scientific principle of proceeding from data to experiment to conclusion, and the stages of the archaeological process must be kept separate when archaeological research is presented for publication. Recording processes are concerned with factual observation and, whenever possible, data are collected by measurement or by reference to agreed standards. Thus archaeological sites are meticulously surveyed and descriptions of objects contain not only words but also photographs, measured drawings, reference to standardised colour charts and, quite often, scientific analyses of their composition.

Not all archaeology is about excavation, although this is a very common misconception; but when excavation is undertaken it is under strictly controlled conditions, which involve recording everything that is removed. Excavation is the ultimate experiment since it is a destructive process which cannot be repeated: once an archaeological feature is removed from the soil it cannot be replaced. Accurate and meticulous recording and measurement should be maintained constantly throughout an excavation. In theory it should be possible to replace any individual artefact in the exact location in which it was found. In practice that is an unattainable ideal – not least because the surrounding archaeological deposits with subtly varying colours of soil, uncontaminated by modern disturbance, would be totally incapable of replication. The destructive nature of excavation causes ethical dilemmas for archaeologists who increasingly see excavation as a last resort and are having more and more recourse to non-invasive techniques for recording and interpreting archaeological sites.

Archaeologists often talk about 'reading' their sites. By this they mean that simultaneously with discovering and recording archaeological evidence they are also interpreting it. Surveys and excavations are always conducted with clear objectives which usually – even when an excavation is being carried out to 'rescue' a site from destruction by natural or human processes – centre round a research question. In scientific terms this research question is the hypothesis which the archaeologist is testing. The process of reading or interpreting the archaeological evidence is what generates the conclusion. In the final published report the evidence base (i.e. the facts which were observed and recorded during the excavation) must be presented separately from the conclusions so that future archaeologists will be able to re-interpret the data – even though they will not be able to repeat the excavation.

What constitutes archaeological evidence is constantly shifting. In the nineteenth century archaeology was essentially about digging things up, and it was the artefacts discovered, whether portable or architectural, which were the prize. 'Follow the walls' and 'on dégage les murs' were catch-phrases of the early excavators. Now, however, archaeology has advanced to the point where even the most minute items are recovered and studied. Thus the tiniest grains of pollen and microscopic plant phytoliths (silicaceous exoskeletal remains), retrieved by fine sieving and flotation techniques, play their part in helping to understand the environmental conditions in which ancient events occurred. It is fair to observe that many of the newer scientific applications used by archaeologists were first applied in prehistoric contexts rather than in relation to Classical sites. It was often claimed that it was pointless, even irresponsible, to use up valuable funding on expensive techniques which would show no more than could be discovered from reading contemporary written accounts. Increasingly, however, archaeologists studying the Classical world are adopting techniques which indicate far, far more about, say, environmental changes than could ever be discerned from the patchy historical record.

Just as the range of evidence exploited has vastly increased, so too have the kinds of questions which the archaeologist is prepared to ask. Formerly the plan of a building or a collection of artefacts were sufficient reward for the labour of excavation. Now for many periods – and the Classical world is one of these – the variety of factual information available is so great that the archaeologist can look beyond the mosaic of data itself to the larger questions of pattern and significance. Often the archaeological record provides a better guide to questions of social structure, of economic development or of commercial relations than historical sources which will almost certainly have a restricted perspective. As with a telescope, where a small, even if distant, feature is seen from a single viewpoint and a whole landscape remains unobserved, a written text conveys the viewpoint of a single author and reflects only those areas he (or very rarely she) found of interest or importance.

Today the archaeologist can look at the location of a building, the quality of the materials used for its construction and decoration and the objects found in association with it to try and determine its likely place in the social hierarchy of the community as a whole. In the same way, the complexity of technology, the proportion of scarce imported materials and the elaboration of the individual objects may reflect the economic prosperity of a town or village. The patterns of distribution of different types of object throughout the Mediterranean – such as Greek and Roman wine amphorae – illuminate not only the trading relations of different regions but the preferences of the customers or the prevailing fashions of different periods. Roman amphorae of republican date found at Hengistbury Head on the south coast of Britain tell us that even before the Roman conquest, the local chieftains had acquired a taste for imported wine and presumably demonstrated their wealth and status by offering it to their guests in preference to locally produced drinks such as beer or mead.

Artefacts may also provide clues about the identity and ethnicity of the different groups within ancient communities – though it has to be admitted that inscriptions such as those on grave stones are often much more explicit. Archaeology has progressed a long way from the former equation of pots and people, the assumption that the use of a particular style of pottery (or other type of artefact) denoted individuals or groups of a particular origin. Now a whole complex of related characteristics from personal ornaments to burial customs and grave forms is needed to support any statement about the origin of a specific group – and even this is made with great caution. Perhaps, before long, DNA testing will remove the need for such speculation.

From here it is but a short step – though a bold one – to try to understand *behaviour* as illustrated by the material remains of an ancient society. Do the ground plans of humble dwellings and grand villas support the often asserted segregation of male and female in the Classical world? How far can the form of the buildings and the finds made be used to identify the activities which took place, whether social, industrial or commercial? Does a repeated pattern of finds at sanctuary sites or in graves illustrate a specific mode of ritual behaviour?

Questions of this kind – though the answers can only ever be tentative and must always be qualified by words like 'possibly' or 'probably' – provide the best chance there is of approaching the psychology of an ancient society and of understanding ancient attitudes or beliefs. Whereas today the natural and supernatural are regarded as separate, unconnected concepts, in the Classical world they were no more than the opposite ends of a continuum of existence and interaction. In formulating answers to such questions, it is vital to bring together again the written and the material evidence, the history and the archaeology, whether they conflict or are complementary.

The term 'Classical' itself is not unproblematic for archaeologists since it can denote a period of time or be used as a cultural or stylistic description. 'Classical' is most commonly used to mean something like 'related to the ancient Greeks and Romans', thus combining chronological and cultural reference. Even so there is a considerable degree of vagueness about the chronological limitations, since purists have applied the term to no more than the fifth and fourth centuries BC, thus excluding the Romans entirely, whilst for others the term can be used to describe anything – event, cultural trend, artistic style, or humble artefact – originating from the Greek and Roman world from at least the sixth century BC to at least the fourth century AD. Classical scholars have also been happy to associate the study of 'Homeric' archaeology with their discipline. This is the world described by the poet Homer, who most probably lived in the eighth century BC, and composed epic poems about events during the Trojan War and its aftermath. The events described by Homer had taken place half a millennium before his time, during a period now known as Mycenaean after its principal site Mycenae, home of the Achaean (Greek) leader Agamemnon. At the other end of the chronological scale, the cut-off point for the end of the Classical period is sometimes taken as the time when Christianity replaced traditional pagan forms as the official religion of the Roman empire in the fourth century BC. This can lead to terminological diversity since whilst, for most classicists, the first four centuries AD are 'Roman imperial', for those interested in the beginnings of Christianity, they are 'early Christian'.

The idea of the 'Classical' is a modern construct. In the medieval period, the Roman empire was seen as surviving until the fall of Christian Constantinople (now Istanbul) to the Islamic Turks in 1453. Those successors of the ancient Greeks and Romans whose capital (founded by Constantine as 'New Rome') this city was, are known today as 'Byzantines'. Ironically, although they were really Greeks, they called themselves 'Romans'. This sort of loose and imprecise terminology is not a huge issue for Classicists dealing with written texts in ancient Greek and Latin, but it is very awkward for archaeologists who need a clear terminology which is specific to a period, and which may often be refined by reference to geography or culture.

Since the work of the Danish scholar Thomsen, who was appointed the first curator of the National Museum in Copenhagen in 1835, archaeologists have referred to broad periods indicated by the level of technological development and the artefacts discovered – the Stone, Bronze or Iron Ages. The Mycenaean period is part of the Bronze Age, whilst the rest of what is termed 'Classical', whether Greek or Roman, falls in the Iron Age. It is important to understand that these terms are vague (sometimes positively unhelpful) since the Iron Age is taken to start in Greece around 1050 BC while in central Europe iron does not come into use until the ninth century BC. In general, the rest of Europe experienced

By	*Greece*	*Near East*	*Italy*	*Britain*
1700	Knossos	Troy		Stonehenge
1600	Shaft Graves; Mycenae	Hittite Empire		
1400	Assiros			
1300	Linear B?			
1200	Trojan War?	Trojan War? Çiftlik		
1000	Assiros	Phoenician alphabet	Urnfield burials	
800	Geometric poetry	Assyrian Empire	Villanovan culture	
700	Homer	Homer; Greek colonies around Black Sea	Greek colonies in S. Italy; foundation of Rome	Hillforts
600	Proto-Corinthian pottery; first coinage	Midas in Phrygia; Persian Empire	Etruscans; Latin Script	Hillforts
500	Peisistratid tyrants at Athens	Darius	Kings expelled; foundation of Republic	Celts Danebury
400	Persian Wars; Athenian Empire; Parthenon; Peloponnesian Wars	Xerxes		
300	Philip of Macedon	Alexander the Great	Gauls sack Rome	Building of Maiden Castle
200	Gauls in Greece	Gauls in Asia Minor	Hannibal invades Italy	
100	Roman sack of Corinth	Pergamum willed to Rome		Oppida and Celtic coinage
0	Sulla sacks Athens; Roman colony at Knossos		Augustus establishes Empire	Hengistbury Head; Caesar's campaigns

Bronze Age — Pre-literate Iron Age

Fig 1.1 From the Mycenaeans to the end of the first century BC.

By	Greece	Near East	Italy	Britain
100	St Paul	St Paul	St Paul; Colosseum; eruption of Vesuvius	Claudius invades; Lunt Fort
200	Temple of Olympian Zeus completed; Pausanias	Jewish diaspora	Trajan's column; Hadrian	Hadrian's Wall; Antonine Wall
300	Gothic invasion; Diocletian	Gothic invasion; Diocletian	Diocletian	Diocletian
400		Foundation of Constantinople; Çiftlik church	Constantine's Edict of Toleration of Christianity	
500	Abolition of Olympic Games	Earthquake at Çiftlik	Alaric sacks Rome; Ravenna	Romans give up Britain
600		Church of St Polyeuktos, Santa Sophia	Ravenna	Bede
700	Slav invasions	Persians and Arabs invade Asia Minor		Sutton Hoo burials
1000	Iconoclasm	Iconoclasm		Vikings
1100	First Crusade	First Crusade; kingdom of Jerusalem	First Crusade	Norman conquest; First Crusade
1200		Richard the Lionheart		Richard the Lionheart
1300	Frankish kingdoms	Crusaders sack Constantinople	Pilastri Acritani brought to Venice	
1400		Ottoman Empire	Petrarch	Black death
1500	Cyriac of Ancona; Turkish conquest	Turkish conquest of Constantinople	Cyriac of Ancona	

Fig 1.2 From the first century AD to the discovery of the New World 1492 AD.

a slower pace of social and technological development than the heartlands of the Greek and Roman world around the Mediterranean basin. This is, of course, part of the context in which the 'civilised' inhabitants of Greece and Italy could regard the peoples of other regions as 'barbarians', criticising them equally for their uncouth languages and 'backward' styles of living.

Archaeologists are also used to attributing types of sites and artefacts which are characteristic of particular areas at particular times to 'cultures'. These are effectively population groups with recognisable traits and habits which can be detected in the physical traces discovered by archaeological means. In this respect, the term 'Classical' is useful for denoting a group of peoples with what archaeologists and anthropologists would recognise as a shared culture. 'Classical' does serve to denote a vibrant culture embracing both Greeks and Romans, with common elements such as can be seen in a range of physical evidence, including town-planning, architecture, burial practices and art as well as a host of portable objects.

For the purposes of this book, then, we have interpreted the term 'Classical' as widely as possible in both chronological and cultural terms, ranging through periods and cultures extending from Mycenaean to late Roman and early Byzantine, and through geographical areas from Britain to Turkey (Figs. 1.1 and 1.2). This is a broad canvas stretching across two millennia and including regions where many different 'cultures' (in the archaeological sense) and many indigenous peoples speaking different languages were brought together in a kaleidoscopic and yet remarkably uniform political community.

The resultant cultural mixes were not one-way processes. Roman culture was deeply influenced by Greek, while the Roman empire assimilated ideas from subject territories ranging from Egypt to Britain as well as spreading Classical influences to them. We speak of 'Roman Britain' as a way of describing Britain under Roman rule, but those who study the archaeology of Roman Britain also use the term Romano-British to describe types of settlement or works of art which display a clear combination of imported Classical elements with native British ones. Classical civilisation thus brought together elements from many different cultures and fused them into a relatively homogeneous and usually very prosperous whole. Archaeologists studying the Classical world profit from the opportunity to see that process in action as shown through a huge variety of types of physical remains.

Chapter 2
The Development of Classical Archaeology

There has surely never been a time since the first appearance of human beings on this planet when the traces of past generations have not been a source of wonder and curiosity. Indeed, the idea of using monuments or other physical evidence to support oral or literary tradition can first be observed in the ancient world. True archaeology, the science of reconstructing the past without the aid of oral or literary sources is, however, a product of the development of a wide range of ideas and techniques within the last 150 years.

2.1 The Classical context

In the Classical world legends about the gods or heroic ancestors were, to those who knew or heard them, 'history' in a very real sense, and it was only gradually that scepticism about the truth of the old stories developed. Even in the middle of the fifth century BC, after many years of 'scientific' enquiry by early Greek philosophers, Herodotus in his *Histories* felt unable to judge the validity of different stories – simply setting them down uncritically as information, sometimes with both sides of the story. Although Thucydides predicted that future generations looking at the paltry physical remains of Sparta would never believe that that city could have been more powerful than Athens which boasted so many magnificent public buildings, the concept of using material remains to corroborate oral tradition (to use modern terms) took many centuries more to develop.

The first evidence of 'antiquarian' interests in the Aegean area comes from Mycenaean Thebes in the thirteenth century BC, where a remarkable hoard of Mesopotamian cylinder seals was found, some already 600 years old at the time they were buried. We cannot explain this ancient collection: were these ancient objects made thousands of kilometres away simply curiosities, or were they thought to have some magical power or religious significance?

There is no doubt that Mycenaean Greeks of the twelfth century BC were well aware of the products of earlier, perhaps more 'heroic', generations. Old tombs received new burials, perhaps to re-establish links with still potent ancestors. By the Archaic period the Mycenaeans had become the heroic Achaean ancestors of Homeric epic and their most familiar monuments – even more then than today – were their great fortresses built with enormous blocks of stone. Believed to be too massive for human hands, their walls were thought of as the work of the Cyclopes, semi-divine giants of legend.

The conscious manipulation of the past for the purposes of the present is well illustrated by Cimon's 'discovery' in the mid-fifth century of the 'bones of Theseus' on the island of Skyros, and their transfer to a new tomb in Athens so that the hero would once again be present to protect his city. The clearance of old tombs from the island of Delos to purify it will have made many workers familiar with old objects; it is hard to imagine that they had no curiosity about what they found. By the late Classical period the habit of recreating Archaic styles of architecture or sculpture to lend antiquity to a new monument can be traced in many places.

The Roman aristocracy had long had a taste for Greek sculpture: Memmius carried off cartloads after the sack of Corinth in 133 BC. When Attalos III of Pergamum stated in his will that he bequeathed his kingdom to Rome, this legacy was taken so literally that works of art were transferred wholesale from Pergamum to Rome and other Italian cities in the last decades of the second century BC, while Sulla continued the process following the sack of Athens early in the first century BC. Even the vast quantities of sculpture in Greek cities and sanctuaries were not enough to satisfy the rapidly expanding demand for ornaments for house and garden, let alone public places, and the art of copying Greek sculpture became a major industry. Examples of such copies intended for shipping to Italy were retrieved from the Piraeus harbour and can now be seen in the archaeological museum there. Pieces of great antiquity were especially prized by collectors and a flourishing 'fine art' market developed in Rome. In the early imperial period (from the second half of the first century BC onwards) art histories were compiled by such scholars as Pliny and Vitruvius while Cicero had already managed to locate the neglected tomb of Archimedes near the city gate of Syracuse.

Despite their proud record of survival and conquest the Romans seem to have suffered from a collective inferiority complex when it came to demonstrating their origins. Almost from the first moment of their involvement in Greek politics, they felt the need to cultivate a heroic past which would be equal, if not actually superior, to that of the Greeks they gradually came to dominate. This process reached a climax in the reign of Augustus with the composition of Vergil's *Aeneid*, among other literary works, and visual realisation in the sculptural reliefs of the *Ara Pacis Augustae* (Altar of the Augustan Peace) where Roman heroic deeds were depicted in Greek style. Subsequent Roman emperors from Caligula to Commodus sought explicit equation of themselves with Greek gods and heroes by having themselves depicted in sculpture as characters like Heracles. The story of the founders of Rome, Romulus and Remus, was regularly depicted on coins and in other art forms (Fig. 2.1)

Fig 2.1 Bronze Sextans, mint of Rome, 217-215 BC. Obverse: She-wolf suckling twins.

As part of the process of integrating the Greek east into the Roman empire Julius Caesar had already taken care to promote ancient Greek cities – and to keep an eye on them – by establishing 'colonies' at Corinth, Troy and Knossos. Knossos and the legends surrounding it, were especially attractive to Roman writers. The ruins of the Bronze Age palace were familiar to later inhabitants. There is no sign that it was ever built over and it may have remained a 'taboo' area in recognition of its connection with the Minotaur and the labyrinth in which it was imprisoned. A curious episode is reported from the reign of Nero in the middle of the first century AD. 'Writing tablets of bark' were discovered in a lead chest at Knossos and taken to Nero – a noted collector as well as musician – who promptly demanded a translation from learned scholars. Failure in this task would doubtless have had a heavy penalty and it is not surprising to learn that they provided a translation. Allegedly they were an account of the exploits of the Cretan hero Idomeneus in the Trojan

War. This sounds like the first report of the Linear B tablets which have contributed so much to our understanding of Bronze Age civilisation – but nothing yet to the story of the heroes outside the walls of Troy. The Knossian connection was taken just as seriously by Nero's successor Galba, who claimed descent from Pasiphae though not from the Minotaur!

Nearly a century later the emperor Hadrian was perhaps the most energetic promoter of Greek heritage, with an enormous programme of building or restoration throughout the Eastern empire – even completing the Temple of Olympian Zeus in Athens, over 600 years after it was started by Peisistratos. This interest in the monuments of past ages prompted the compilation of what may be thought of as the earliest surviving traveller's handbook, Pausanias' account of his travels in Greece written about AD 150. This records visits to many of the sites and monuments of central and southern Greece with descriptions of what could still be seen, and what had been lost, together with the stories told by their guardians about their construction or the legends associated with them. Much is reported uncritically and in places one can detect – as in some of its modern counterparts – the description of sites Pausanias had not visited for himself. He does, however, from time to time, cite the evidence for an identification, the dedicatory inscription or some similar feature. For many sites his work remains a vital source of information for archaeologists studying the Classical world, providing the only clues towards the identification of buildings of which no more than the foundations still survive.

With the rise of Christianity and its adoption as the official religion of the Roman empire by Constantine in the fourth century AD, the monuments to the old gods were increasingly neglected, converted into churches, or, by the fifth century, positively obliterated. A different kind of heritage was honoured or sought – the relics of the martyrs and early church fathers, the places where they taught, were imprisoned or martyred, and most prized of all, their very bones. The fourth, fifth and sixth centuries AD saw the construction of a vast number of splendid basilical churches throughout the eastern Roman empire, often marking the (alleged) sites of some memorable event. These basilicas represent one of the last great manifestations of Roman architecture and were decorated with mosaics, wall-paintings and architectural sculpture in thoroughly Classical style. The remains of many of these early churches can still be seen in Turkey, Syria and north Africa, though most were replaced as Byzantine architecture developed a new style from the seventh century onwards, and others, especially in the western Roman empire, were destroyed during the barbarian invasions and the frequent earthquakes of the sixth and seventh centuries.

The disintegration of the western part of the empire, which accelerated during the fifth century AD, was followed by the long period until the end of the tenth century when curiosity was certainly not dead but the crumbling monuments of former pagan times were merely part of the landscape. These ruins provided convenient quarries for building materials or sculptured decoration. The only materials from the Classical world which were still regularly prized were the manuscripts preserving works of literature or medicine, philosophy or Christian theology. These were jealously guarded in the monasteries and more or less accurately copied or transcribed. Even more of the literary and scientific heritage of ancient Greece was preserved by the Arabs, who had gradually gained control of the eastern Mediterranean as the Byzantine Empire, in its turn, succumbed to the attacks of more vigorous neighbours to the south and east.

2.2 Looters, antiquarians and collectors: from the Middle Ages to Elgin

Surviving descriptions of antiquities are few and far between but among the earliest are itineraries listing the holy places of Rome where the ancient ruins were used as landmarks. Soon, however, it became the fashion for wealthy men such as Henry of Blois, Bishop of Winchester, who visited Rome around 1150, to build up collections of ancient statues – to prevent the contemporary Romans from renewing their idolatrous worship of them! Architectural or sculptural fragments, especially columns, were regularly sought to embellish new buildings – a practice which alarmed some authorities. Edicts began to be issued for the preservation of specific monuments. In 1162, for example, the Roman Senate threatened capital punishment for anyone who damaged Trajan's column. More often, however, the Roman monuments were simply used as quarries of building materials, regardless of threats or penalties.

Travel between east and west was infrequent and it was only at the end of the tenth century that pilgrimage to Jerusalem became more regular. The Crusades, started in 1095 to preserve the right of pilgrimage, greatly increased first-hand knowledge of the eastern Mediterranean. Interest at first still focussed largely on Christian relics – the bones of saints or fragments of the true cross – enough of the latter, apparently, to forest a medium-sized island.

Byzantine emperors continued to seek the support of the Pope in Rome to maintain the foothold in the Holy Land won in 1098, but the fortunes of the Crusaders were mixed and the opposition stiff. Booty became as important as the original goal of personal absolution through pilgrimage, and an easy victim lay to hand: the Byzantine capital Constantinople with the accumulated wealth and treasures of centuries. The Knights of the fourth Crusade never reached the coast of Palestine but stopped to sack Constantinople in 1204 and to partition what remained of the Byzantine empire among themselves. Works of art, precious materials and ancient manuscripts were once again shipped wholesale from east to west and wealthy patrons in northern Italy, and in Venice in particular, became familiar with Greek sculpture. The best known examples of this process are the bronze horses which now adorn St. Mark's

Cathedral in Venice. Much of the architectural sculpture which is a feature of St. Mark's Square was also lifted from buildings in Constantinople (Fig. 2.2). These acquisitions stimulated the search for examples still buried in northern Italy, and we learn that in 1240 the Holy Roman Emperor Frederick II issued a licence for an excavation near Augusta in the expectation of *inventiones maximas* – major discoveries.

The prosperity and stability of northern Italy during the thirteenth and fourteenth centuries stimulated art and scholarship at a period when some of the world's first universities were established. Manuscripts were transcribed and discussed, classical sculpture was copied or adapted, and the monuments themselves began to be recorded. Giovanni Mansionario, an official of the cathedral in Verona who died in 1337, added descriptions and diagrams of theatres and circuses and illustrations of ancient coins to his manuscripts. Between 1310 and 1330 Benzo d'Alessandria compiled an encyclopaedia with frequent references to antiquities and inscriptions. Petrarch, best known as the leading Latin scholar of his age who edited texts of Vergil, Livy and Cicero, first visited Rome in 1337 and enthusiastically explored the ruins of its past glory in the expectation of identifying the sites of episodes related,

Fig 2.2 The 'pilastri acritani', so-called because of a supposed association with Acre in the Holy Land, were actually removed by Crusaders from the sixth-century Church of St. Polyeuktos in Constantinople nearly a thousand years after it was built.

for example, by Livy. He was often mistaken but his work marks one of the earliest attempts to combine the study of history and monuments which today underlies every aspect of Classical archaeology.

The Renaissance of the fifteenth century – the rebirth of art and culture the equal of the ancients – saw an explosion of interest in Classical literature and inscriptions, architecture and sculpture. Biondo, in the service of the Pope at Rome from 1433 onwards, was perhaps the scholar most devoted in his time to the pursuit of what today we would call archaeology. He compiled an archaeological handbook of surviving remains and attempted reconstructions of life in his massive work *Roma instaurata* – Rome restored. Inscriptions, coins, monuments, texts and archives were all drawn together in compiling a rational account of the ancient city. The first reported underwater archaeology belongs to the same period – the unsuccessful attempt to raise two Roman ships, from the bottom of Lake Nemi, which were finally salvaged in 1935. A little earlier Cristoforo Buondelmonti had reported an impressive collection of ancient Greek statues in the garden of the country house of a Venetian noble settled in Crete (by then under Venetian control): statues which probably originated from the Roman colony of Knossos or the capital of the island, Gortyn.

Curiosity must been aroused in many others by this fresh awareness of the antique world, but we know of only one whose curiosity was spurred into systematic action beyond Italy. Cyriac of Ancona (born 1391) was a merchant who spent nearly 30 years in Greece and the Levant in the first half of the fifteenth century visiting libraries and monuments (Fig. 2.3). Conscious of the speed with which quarrying was destroying ancient ruins, he lost no opportunity to record what he saw in words and sketches, visiting obscure sites as well as the well-known centres. His work is a landmark in the history of archaeology: his records, though imperfect, are the first to attempt a systematic account of Greek monuments and inscriptions since Pausanias over a thousand years earlier.

The fall of Constantinople in 1453 and the capture of Greece by the Turks between 1453 and 1458 brought renewed isolation but in no way diminished the enthusiasm for Classical art. Mantegna (1431-1506) was perhaps the greatest of the artists of this period who employed reasonably authentic monuments as backgrounds for their studies of biblical episodes or peopled their scenes with characters borrowed from ancient sculpture. Collectors had to make do with objects found in Italy for the most part, copying and 'restoring' them just as their ancestors had done fifteen hundred years earlier. In many cases these were personal collections, like those of Pope Paul II or Lorenzo de' Medici, and dispersed after their deaths (1471 and 1492 respectively). It was Pope Sixtus IV (Paul II's successor) who provided the impetus which established the marvellous Vatican and Capitoline collections, including the famous bronze statue of the she-wolf suckling the twins Romulus and Remus which can still be seen on the Capitoline Hill (Fig. 2.4). This is an excellent example of the fashions of the time, since the fifth century BC bronze statue of the wolf is supplemented by a pair of Renaissance babies to complete the story.

Fig 2.3 At the end of the fifteenth century the architect Guiliano San Gallo made an accurate copy of some of Cyriac of Ancona's own drawings. Cyriac had visited Oeniadae in western Mainland Greece in 1436 and recorded, as seen here, the remains of its walls and the remarkable ship-sheds where trieremes were pulled up out of the water for maintenance or over-wintering. Cyriac's report of the buttresses cut from the living rock – integer lapis – was only confirmed four-and-a-half centuries later when excavation started in 1900. Even then it took the excavators some time to find the inscribed name Aristidas he included in his sketch. Today few tourists visit this remote and once impregnable site.

Despite this awareness of an ancient past all around them, the authorities of the sixteenth century in Italy and elsewhere had no scruples about demolishing monuments or robbing them. At Rome, for example, the pyramid long known (erroneously) as Romulus' tomb was pulled down in 1499 to make way for a new road. A few years later, in 1525, Pope Urban VIII was responsible for stripping the bronze sheeting from the roof of the portico of the Pantheon in the hope that it was suitable for making cannon (it was not!). The appointment by Pope Paul III of a commissioner for antiquities in 1534 did little to slow the pace of destruction. The monuments were steadily disappearing as collection gathered momentum all over Europe.

The work of Andrea Palladio published in 1570 marks a milestone in the study of Classical architecture. In his meticulous drawings of surviving buildings such as the Pantheon, he consciously sought to reveal the principles of proportion and construction as set out by the Roman writer Vitruvius. The ground plans and elevations of real or imaginary Roman buildings provided architects for generations to come with the inspiration for Palladian neoclassical buildings through the length and breadth of Europe.

By the beginning of the seventeenth century travellers on the Grand Tour to complete their gentleman's education began to visit Classical lands regularly, collecting whenever permitted and sometimes recording what they saw. King Charles I and the Earl of Arundel were among those in England who assembled collections of material, principally sculpture, brought back in this way. The Ottoman empire was now more open and the Venetians still maintained footholds in Crete and other places. Among the most important records of this century are the detailed publications by Spon and Wheler (1675-6) of antiquities seen in both

Fig 2.4 Bronze statue of the she-wolf with the twins Romulus and Remus added nearly 2000 years later.

Greece and Asia Minor and the fullest record of the then still intact Parthenon reliefs and pediments in drawings by Carrey (1674). At the same time the skills of surveying and the basics of most of the necessary instruments were perfected (Chapter 4).

Access to sites was often difficult and misidentifications were common, but progress in recording continued in the eighteenth century, rapidly spurred on by the scholarship of Winckelmann who identified the main stages of Greek art and showed how Roman art was derived and developed from it. The discovery at the beginning of the century of Herculaneum and Pompeii under the volcanic ash of Mt Vesuvius brought to light a wealth of wall-painting and mosaics, bronze statues and domestic items. In England, antiquaries such as Stukeley pursued Roman remains with enthusiasm, even noting the value of crop marks for revealing the existence of buried buildings.

In Athens, the architects Stuart and Revett spent four years from 1751-5 making meticulous measured drawings which could be used as inspiration for fashionable country houses and chateaux in the classical style. They even undertook excavation to reach the foundations of several buildings and complete the drawing of the elevations. The newly established Society of Dilettanti sponsored similar studies by Chandler in Asia Minor between 1764 and 1766 when he made detailed records of the cities of Miletus and Didyma, Ephesus and Priene, among many others.

Collection remained the primary aim and ambassadors were often well placed to achieve it. Hamilton collected and published Greek and South Italian vases – providing the material for Wedgwood's classical ceramic designs. Choiseul-Gouffier sent the painter Fauvel to Athens with specific instructions to 'remove everything you can'. This had the result that several pieces of the Parthenon sculptures are now to be found in the Louvre. The most notorious of these collectors – many would say the most rapacious – was Elgin, who in 1801 obtained a firman (permit) from the Turkish authorities to copy and remove sculpture from the Acropolis. His agents Lusieri and Hunt were so successful that the majority of the surviving Parthenon marbles were removed and shipped to London. Even at the time the ethics of Elgin's action were questioned, while the ownership of the Parthenon marbles remains a matter of dispute between the Greek government and the British Museum.

2.3 The 'gold rush' years: excavation or archaeology?

At first, excavation had been undertaken solely for the purpose of discovering portable objects to fill the 'cabinets of curiosities' of elegant noblemen, but the interest in Classical architecture, which had developed in the eighteenth century, soon prompted systematic excavation which was carried out to increase knowledge, i.e. for research purposes.

In Rome, Pope Pius VII instigated the clearance and restoration of many monuments from 1800 on and this work was continued with remarkable energy and substantial cost by a commission set up under the Napoleonic government of the city between 1809 and 1813. Work on the Forum, Colosseum, Arch of Titus, Basilica of Maxentius and the Pantheon, among many other buildings, dates to this period and details of the work force and materials required are all documented in the accounts of the state archive.

In Greece the first systematic excavations occurred at Aegina where the temple of Aphaia was explored (1811) and at Bassae where an international expedition, whose best known members were Cockerell and von

Stackelberg, cleared the whole of the temple (1812). Both teams made careful records of their work but the best finds were still exported – to Munich and London respectively.

Greek independence in 1829 not only brought the export of major finds to a halt but also the appointment of the first curator of antiquities in Athens and, not long after, the formation of the Greek Archaeological Society. Exploration and export still continued, however, in Asia Minor where Newton excavated at Cnidos and uncovered the Mausoleum at Halicarnassus, preparing detailed publications of both.

Wood worked less systematically at Ephesus in the 1860s in the search for the Temple of Artemis but he, or rather his assistant Corporal Trotman, should be given the credit for the first use of photography on an archaeological site in the Aegean area (Fig. 2.5). The great religious sanctuaries of the Classical world provided some of the most alluring opportunities for treasure-hunting, but at the same time techniques of stratigraphic excavation began to be developed, albeit somewhat coarsely and some years after their first employment in Britain. Curtius' work at Olympia and Conze's at Samothrace were models of their kind, paying attention to the sequence of the different phases at well as to the architecture and finds. Excavations at Pompeii, Delos, Pergamum, the Acropolis at Athens, Corinth, Miletus and Delphi followed, to name but a few of the Classical sites explored by the end of the nineteenth century. Some were well conducted, others little more than treasure hunts.

Between 1870 and 1890 Heinrich Schliemann, the father of prehistoric archaeology in the Aegean, had directed his attention to Troy and Mycenae among other sites of Homeric legend. He was convinced that the epics were based on historical events and he had the personal fortune which enabled him to try and demonstrate this through excavation. At first he showed limited concern for stratigraphy and minimal respect for the local authorities. His large work force was driven to cut through level after level at Troy in the expectation of finding buildings and treasure worthy of king Priam, and Schliemann's finds of gold were smuggled out of Turkey at dead of night. But he was nothing if not a fast learner and both learnt by experience and sought expert help. He enlisted Dörpfeld, for example, an architect who had learnt his archaeology at Olympia and who continued to excavate at Troy after Schliemann's death, resolving many of the problems relating to its interpretation and chronology. Schliemann's discovery of the Mycenaean palace at Tiryns as well as the Shaft Graves at Mycenae encouraged many others to turn their attention to this period.

The credit for introducing stratigraphic excavation to Greece can perhaps best be given to a Scottish architect, Mackenzie, who explored the prehistoric settlement at Phylakopi on the island of Melos between 1896 and 1899 and established standards of excavation and recording well ahead of most of his contemporaries. These skills were put to great use from 1900 on at Knossos, where Sir Arthur Evans employed him as his principal assistant. Mackenzie deserves much of the credit for keeping

Fig 2.5 Corporal Trotman's photograph of Wood's excavation of the Temple of Artemis at Ephesus in 1860.

the record at Knossos straight, though it was Evans who had the vision to pursue King Minos into his palace.

On the whole, until this point, the pursuit of the past in the museum or in the field had been a male domain. Fierce remarks were made by such as J.P. Droop as late as 1915 about the 'proprieties' and the constraints which might arise in the presence of women on an excavation. As in so many areas, however, the revolution was well under way. Lady Hester Stanhope had travelled indefatigably in the Near East at the beginning of the nineteenth century, visiting Palmyra and eventually settling in Syria. Schliemann encouraged his Greek wife Sophia to take a full part in the excavations at Troy and in Greece. In the first decade of the twentieth century Esther Boise Van Deman embarked on a detailed study of the standing monuments of Rome, Harriet Boyd Hawes explored eastern Crete and laid bare the Minoan town of Gournia, while Gertrude

Bell set off into the heart of Anatolia equipped with camel and camera to record the monuments of every age. To the same period belongs the appointment of one of the greatest experts on Classical sculpture, Gisela Richter, to the Metropolitan Museum in New York.

Fig 2.6 Reconstructing the Lunt fort. The Royal Engineers erecting the gateway.

2.4 Archaeology comes of age: the twentieth century

By the beginning of the twentieth century the foundations of archaeology in the Classical lands were well laid. Most periods had been explored somewhere and most areas of the eastern Mediterranean had received some attention. Local scholars had begun to play a role as important as that of their better resourced colleagues from America and Austria, Britain, France and Germany and Russia. The first half of the twentieth century can be seen as a period of consolidation: apart from the interruptions caused by two major wars, research and publication continued steadily, while typologies and chronologies were established and set out as the basis for further study. Excavation was usually archaeological, though standards varied, and it was normally directed to the solution of a problem rather than the simple discovery of a new monument or to a search for objects for museum display. Excavation procedures developed very rapidly and excavators became much more reflective about their methods. A very major contribution to establishment of excavation as a scientific process was made by Sir Mortimer Wheeler, who perfected his techniques at a variety of British sites such as Maiden Castle during the 1920s and 30s.

After the Second World War, however, approaches radically changed as urban and industrial development promoted more and more rescue excavation, as new scientific techniques became available and as new philosophies in the interpretation of the finds began to be applied to the results. Sponsors are now more often universities or government funds rather than wealthy patrons, and cost-effectiveness has become ever more important. Old sites continue to be revisited with fresh results while new sites have provided new perspectives on the old. Classical archaeology as an aspect of art history chiefly concerned with vase-paintings and architecture has begun to yield to the much wider study of the archaeology of the Classical world. Classical archaeology is now seen as providing a mass of information which is often complementary to the literary or historical sources rather than dependent on them. Work in the prehistoric field, less bound by preconceptions, has often led the way.

Intensive survey of a landscape is now a well established method applied in many areas to reveal the changing patterns of land use and settlement. Mapping techniques from aerial photography to satellite imaging and geo-positioning techniques all speed up the process of recording. Geographical and environmental studies, both on- and off-site, are now standard methods of understanding landscape changes or human exploitation of plant and animal resources. Geophysical survey, employing resistivity and magnetometry techniques, can speed up the process of locating buildings or even map a settlement plan without excavation. Rigorous stratigraphic excavation and detailed recording is now the norm rather than the exception. It is expected that all finds will be studied and published in detail, though some would say that the achievement rate is still too low!

Many new techniques exist for making the most of the objects found, ranging from dating techniques such as Carbon 14 or dendrochronology (see Chapter 7.4) to analysis by chemical or spectrographic means in order to determine the composition of pottery or other materials – and thus perhaps their provenance and the manufacturing processes employed, as well as the consumable products which the pottery object contained. Computer-based techniques enable the processing of large quantities of data rapidly and therefore create the possibility of making quantitative comparisons between different periods or areas.

The interpretation of finds and results has become much more rigorous, employing behavioural models derived from human geography or anthropology against which the data collected through excavation or survey can be tested. Presentation of results to the public through museum and site exhibitions (Fig. 2.6) and in educational programmes is now of a very high standard. The problems of the long term conservation of sites and monuments are being steadily addressed so that they will, hopefully, survive another two thousand years of decay resulting from human and natural causes.

New sites are explored almost every day but few are as remarkable as the city of Akrotiri on Thera, covered by volcanic ash around 1600 BC; the tomb of Philip II of Macedon (murdered in 332 BC) at Vergina with its rich grave offerings and wall-paintings; or the remains of the ancient lighthouse at Alexandria, gradually being explored on the sea bed. Major developments in the great cities of Europe are now more regulated, with much more attention being given to archaeological remains disturbed, for instance, by the building of the Athens Metro or the re-development of the City of London. The globalisation of archaeology, first perhaps seen in the international efforts to raise monuments like the Trajanic temple at Philae in Egypt which was flooded by the Aswan dam, has resulted in multinational initiatives to identify world heritage sites and to rescue threatened archaeological monuments like the site of the Classical city of Zeugma in eastern Turkey – much of the funding for which has come from the multinational Hewlett-Packard corporation, demonstrating a new switch in the nature of archaeological sponsorship.

Chapter 3
Project Development

3.1 Problem-oriented research

Every field project is different – a unique experiment conducted under scientific principles but unrepeatable. There is no longer any room for the 'let's dig a hole and see what we find' school of exploration so characteristic of work in the nineteenth century. Preliminary research and planning are essential, whether the project is a rescue one or a targeted piece of research. Whether the work involves destructive excavation or non-destructive survey and recording, the results obtained will be much more significant if the questions to be addressed are carefully formulated and the likely answers are considered in advance. In the present climate of limited resources – of money or manpower – every stage of an archaeological project needs to be carefully planned, costed and justified. This problem-oriented approach will apply whether the project arises from research or rescue: a strategy must be developed which will convince research funding councils or local authority planners and developers that the work is essential, and is properly planned, appropriately staffed, and reasonably costed.

Problem-oriented field research may take many forms:

- survey of a landscape to determine the density and history of settlement;

- exploration of a town or village by both survey and excavation to enable understanding of its plan and perhaps its social organisation;

- uncovering of a single building such as a theatre or church to determine its architecture and history;

- excavation of a cemetery to recover information about demographics and social ranking on the basis of the skeletal remains and the 'grave goods' with the burials;

- excavation of a deep site with a long history to provide a 'key' to the relative chronology of a number of smaller, shallower sites;

- recovery of a representative selection of artefacts of pottery, metal or stone to enable the relationship between different areas or regions to be determined;

- systematic sampling of environmental remains during excavation to cast light on the farming and crop processing practices which have underpinned almost every human society since the beginning of the Neolithic period.

It is equally important to prepare for the unexpected – neither human behaviour nor archaeological discovery are wholly predictable, and the one depends entirely on the other. While each field project will start with one or two well defined goals, the accidents of discovery may well change the emphasis during a single season's work or require new approaches depending on the preservation of the remains. The walls of the Roman villa it was planned to explore may have been robbed away, for example, while a mediaeval pottery kiln found alongside offers an entirely new perspective on a different period. The excavator must be well prepared – for the unexpected as well as the anticipated discoveries – and be able to take tactical decisions about priorities as the whole picture or, as often, parts of several different pictures, begin to emerge.

Provision must also be made for what happens after the excavation: it is just as unacceptable today to leave discoveries and sites exposed to weather and degradation as it is to leave boxes and bags of finds in the corner of some makeshift storeroom with no thought for study or publication.

Rescue projects have a rather different set of problems to be addressed. The site is already chosen but the excavator/surveyor entrusted with the recovery before development may well have to decide which parts should be explored or what proportion of the whole sampled. Such decisions will be easier to make if as much research and preparation as time and resources allow is undertaken in advance. The developers and contractors, whatever the nature of the project, will have their own agenda and their own timescale. The archaeologist needs to understand this agenda from the outset, so that planning can be appropriately carried out and so that any request for variation of the developer's timetable (and the financial implications of delay) can be taken into account when requests are made for changes in plan because of unexpected finds. All members of the European Union have legislation requiring adequate investigation of the 'environmental impact' before planning permission is granted – investigation which must be carried out at the developer's expense. Implementation of this legislation is variable and in some cases subject to political interference when, for example, an urgent Government project might be delayed or modified. Such rescue projects may arise from housing developments or improvements to the rail and road networks, or from flooding resulting from hydro-electric schemes. Once the plans for rescue and research have been drawn up with the planning authority and agreed with the developer, changes can only be made with difficulty. The discoveries will need to be of outstanding quality before the work can be held up or the road diverted. Compromise is usually essential – along with excellent public relations. The occasional preservation of parts of Roman London in the basements of new office blocks has only been achieved with goodwill and public and private benefactions. There is no legislation which automatically ensures the preservation of buildings, however important.

A second aspect of planning rescue projects is the study of the finds. Full publication of the finds and results is just as important as if the project was research-oriented – but strong persuasion may be needed to convince those who are paying of the level of effort and expenditure this requires. A convincing argument is easier to muster if there has been thorough preliminary research.

Some projects may be museum-based: this type of work may include the 'excavation' of data neglected for decades or the re-examination of material housed in a wide variety of places, whether previously fully or partly published. Such projects require no less planning and preparation for all stages of the work from permissions to publication: the careful definition of the problems to be addressed will not only aid the progress of the work but also the search for funding.

3.2 Background research

Background research is essential to the success of every project. It may well arise from the general training or experience the leader has gained through years of working as an assistant or from personal research in a specific field. One of the many questions asked before deciding about funding or permits is whether the project leader – and often his staff – are suitably qualified. Long gone are the days reflected in the guidelines to students published in an early volume of the *Annual of the British School at Athens*, when a student of Classical archaeology was deemed ready to conduct his first independent excavation during his second year in Greece. (The concept of her first independent research was hardly to be countenanced.)

Whatever the starting point, the preliminary procedures are likely to be similar. Assuming that an appropriate site has yet to be located for the project to be carried out, there must first be a thorough review of the present state of knowledge, using the resources of libraries, museums and archives. In order to gain as wide a perspective as possible – not only on the likely discoveries and results, but also on those unexpected 'bonuses' which often come the way of the archaeologist these studies will take into account such sources of information as:

- historical or archaeological overviews of the area or period in which the project will be set;

- previous work on sites of similar character whether in the same area or further afield, (published as site reports or archived for later reference);

- historical or literary sources describing the area at any point in the past;

- documents or inscriptions from the proposed study area;

- examination of topographical and geological maps and aerial photographs;

- examination of visible remains on site;

- examination of artefacts in museum collections.

The second stage of preparing for the project is to visit likely sites to assess their suitability on both archaeological and practical grounds. There is no point, for example, in expecting to excavate Minoan levels at Knossos in areas where they are covered by three metres of Hellenistic and Roman deposits. Although it may have been acceptable in the days of Schliemann or Evans to dig through such later levels hurriedly to achieve what seemed then a more important goal, this ignored the contribution that remains of all periods have to make to our knowledge of the past. Today, and rightly so, the destruction of the buildings of one period to reveal those of another requires considerable justification and permission to do so is obtained only with great difficulty.

The character of the site selected will also have considerable bearing on the planning stage: as shown in chapter 5, every type of site has its own special problems and potential, ranging from the depth and stability of the deposits on the one hand to the availability of shade or a water supply on the other.

It is just as important to consider such mundane matters as providing accommodation for the project team, food for them to eat and working areas for the study and safe-keeping of finds made. Rewarding archaeological sites have a habit of being located in remote places and the archaeologist, no less than Napoleon's army, marches on her (just as much as on his) stomach. Will transport be needed from a local town or village where accommodation can be rented, or will a tented encampment with cook house and lavatories be the only solution? All these considerations will affect the choice of site and size and duration of the project which in turn determine the costings.

3.3 Project design

No successful archaeological project can be carried out without spending a substantial amount of time on the detailed planning and administration, especially when it is to take place a long way from home. From the first discussion with colleagues and collaborators about a potential project the team is immediately faced with the daunting prospect of designing a project plan, of raising funds, of gaining permission from the relevant authorities, and often of transporting people and equipment many hundreds of kilometres to operate in both an unfamiliar climate and culture.

A detailed project design is, of course, essential in order for the project to run smoothly and attract funding. It encourages the project director to consider every aspect of the proposed research from both academic and administrative perspectives; it also acts as a means of keeping the team members properly informed. Funding institutions lay great stress on the formulation of, and adherence to, a strict project design. Even if a project is intended to continue for many years (for example, 25 years of excavations are planned at the Neolithic site of Çatalhöyük in Turkey), five-year planning phases are strongly encouraged for major excavation projects, while three-year plans may be applicable to less ambitious survey projects. All post-fieldwork elements and publication preparation must be factored into the project structure and timetable. Even if the project is of limited duration (perhaps a one-year project to study some artefacts held in a museum) a funding institution will still wish to see an outline of the project timetable and plan. The importance of the project plan cannot be over-emphasised. For example, the British Institute of Archaeology at Ankara insists that the directors of all new projects complete a project proposal form; failure to do so will lead to disqualification from funding opportunities.

Academic considerations

The project plan must be as explicit and specific as possible about the research questions, objectives and methods of the project. Funding institutions will give particular encouragement to research directed towards well-defined and realistically achievable goals. Using the excavation of the church at Çiftlik in northern Turkey as an example, research questions, objectives and methods could be expressed as follows.

Research questions:

- What can we discern about the architectural form and detail of the church?
- What date can be established for the construction, occupation and destruction of the church?
- How does material from Çiftlik relate to contemporary material from Asia Minor and the provinces bordering the Black Sea?

Research objectives:

- Produce a plan of the church and analyse its phases of usage;
- Record all finds;
- Protect the site from further damage;
- Conserve the mosaic;
- Publish a complete report.

Research methods:

- Excavate and survey the church;
- Record all finds on an electronic database; photograph and draw a selection of finds;
- Construct and maintain a wall to protect the site from erosion from the sea;
- Stabilise and protect the mosaic;
- Publish the project as a monograph with contributions from team members.

In addition, as much detail as possible must be provided about the post-fieldwork and publication programmes, bearing in mind that these elements must be fully integrated within the project structure. Thus the post-fieldwork and publication work outlined for each year of the project plan must reflect the fieldwork proposed for that year. For example, if the fieldwork scheme includes the intention to survey a particular structure, then the post-fieldwork element must include the production of the plan of the structure and, if it is intended to include this particular plan in the final publication, it must be produced to the necessary publication standard.

Administrative considerations

Every field project, whether based around survey or excavation, has to balance academic outcomes against the practicalities of execution, but the order in which decisions must be taken in preparing the design are generally very similar (even if some have been taken out of the hands of the archaeologist by financial, environmental or political circumstances).

- *What are the overall goals for this project?*
Field survey or excavation or both?
Research or rescue?
Re-burial or display of structures after excavation?

- *What issues affect the achievement of these goals?*
Archaeological method: deep trenches, shallow area excavation?
Practical: soft sand or masses of fallen masonry?
Environmental conditions. Urban or rural? Dry or wet? Hot or cold?

- *How do we secure the best balance of resource and effort to achieve these goals?*
Machine excavation or pick and shovel work for initial clearance?
What level of recording?

- *Taking account of local conditions and available resources, what should be the composition and balance of the site team?*
Hired local workmen, paid archaeologists, student volunteers, experienced supervisors, specialists in planning or photography, specialists in environmental recovery.

- *Where and when should finds processing be conducted?*
In parallel with fieldwork or after it?
On-site or in the finds depot?
How much storage and working space is required?

- *How should the finds team be composed?*
Finds cataloguing specialists, conservator, draughtsman, ceramic specialist, numismatist, bones specialist, palaeobotanist?

- *What support team is needed?*
Housekeeper, cook, secretary, IT technician?

- *What equipment/materials are needed?*
Tools for use on site: spades, trowels, buckets, sieves, etc.
Items for finds collection on site: trays, bags, etc.

Photographic equipment/materials: cameras, lenses, tripods, scales, film, etc.

Recording equipment: tapes, measures, stationery, notebooks, drawing boards, etc.

Equipment for specialist activities such as geophysical prospecting or very fine sieves to retrieve environmental samples.

Household supplies for rented accommodation or for camping.

- *Should equipment be bought, borrowed or hired?*

It is usually simplest to purchase basic equipment like spades and buckets though sometimes these can be borrowed from, or shared with, local museums or other projects operating at different times. Some experts may bring their own equipment (e.g. cameras). Expensive pieces of equipment for surveying will probably have to be hired. Very few excavators can justify the purchase of earth-moving machines, though a vehicle for transporting equipment and team members may be a sensible purchase.

- *What is the most effective way to arrange travel to foreign sites?*

Taking account of time and expense is it better to pay for air fares or for long-distance vehicle travel?

- *What are the best ways to arrange local transport and accommodation?*

Is public transport available or suitable? Is it better to camp on site (saves time and transport costs) or rent accommodation in a nearby town where there are superior facilities?

- *How should we protect the site during an excavation?*

Do we need to hire a guard? Is there secure fencing? Does the site need protection from natural forces (erosion, flood, etc)?

- *How will post-excavation study be facilitated?*

Is sufficient funding built into the project budget? How much can be conducted in the UK, and how much will need to be conducted subsequently on-site or in the finds depot?

- *How will publication be secured?*

Are appropriate experts available? Is there necessary funding for (e.g.) illustrations? What form will publication take – book, article in a journal, internet?

- *How will the site be presented and/or conserved after excavation?*

Will the site be left open or covered up? Are there sources of funding for presentation and display? If the site is to be consolidated and left open for viewing, are there sustainable sources of funding to cover maintenance and security?

Each of these decisions will have financial implications which must be incorporated in a budget. Potential funding institutions will expect to see as much detail as possible. As well as fieldwork costs, all relevant post-fieldwork elements and publication preparation must also be included in the budget (see Fig. 3.2).

An excavation team will usually require all, or most, of the personnel set out in Fig. 3.1. The total number of individuals involved will, of course,

PLANNING	FIELDWORK	POST-FIELDWORK	PUBLICATION
Project director	Project director	Project director	Project director
Administrator	Administrator	Senior archaeologist	Senior archaeologist
	Senior archaeologist	Conservator	Surveyor
	Archaeologist(s)	Surveyor	Finds supervisor
	Surveyor	Finds supervisor	Finds specialists
	Surveying assistant	Finds specialists	Illustrator
	Finds supervisor	Illustrator	IT/clerical assistant
	Finds assistant		
	Finds specialists (e.g. pottery, bones, flora)		
	Illustrator		
	Conservator		
	Photographer		
	Representatives of government and/or local museums		

Fig. 3.1 Typical staffing requirements for different stages of an excavation project.

vary depending on the size and nature of the site and the fieldwork planned for any particular year. The largest teams to work at Çiftlik have been assembled in the years when excavation, surveying, geological assessment and conservation aspects of the project were being conducted simultaneously. They comprised thirteen to fifteen people from the UK, two archaeologists from the Sinop Museum, plus a locally hired work force of up to forty people consisting of workmen, finds washers, and assistants to bring water and make tea, this last being as necessary a commodity for the local workforce as for the British team! At Assiros the larger seasons needed a team of thirty archaeologists and students, with another twenty locally employed for excavation and washing finds.

A survey project focussed on a previously identified site will normally require a smaller team. In addition to the project director and a surveyor, one would expect the team to comprise surveying assistants, a finds supervisor, draughtsman and a photographer. Specialists would probably be limited to an expert in the pottery of the site. For an area survey, however, (i.e. a project with the objective of identifying sites of a range of periods throughout a geographic region) a larger team is required. In addition to the staff listed for a single-site survey, a number of general assistants are required to conduct field-walking across large areas of land in order to collect and record surface finds.

3.4 The legal framework

Before any archaeological work can be undertaken the project director will need to secure permission from the relevant authorities. Obtaining a permit for work in a foreign country can be a very lengthy affair, so that he or she should generally be thinking at least a year ahead. Naturally each country has its own legislative provision which determines the framework within which excavation may be carried out and which determines the ultimate ownership of the finds made.

In Britain and Western Europe, the long tradition of amateur archaeology developed in the context of minimal controls. In Britain permission of the land owner was the sole prerequisite for excavation, except where the site was already designated as a scheduled ancient monument permission for research would have to be given by the government agency responsible – currently English Heritage for sites in England. The finds usually belong to the land owner, except where this right has been waived in favour of a museum or other institution. In Britain, too, there is the particular law of 'treasure trove' relating to valuable finds which have been discovered, often accidentally, centuries after their original owner (who cannot now be identified) lost or hid them. In such circumstances the crown can claim rights to the finds, but an inquest must be held to determine ownership formally.

In practice today research-based fieldwork and excavation in Britain may be carried out by University or museum-based archaeologists, while rescue excavations are usually the province of Field Units – commercial organisations largely funded by the contract work they carry out for developers. Many local authorities now employ planning archaeologists whose job it is to vet planning applications for their impact on known or potential archaeological deposits. Controlled archaeological evaluation can be imposed as a planning condition, and the results of such evaluations are typically deposited in the relevant Sites and Monuments Records (SMR) offices.

In the Mediterranean the long tradition, both legal and illegal, of export of finds has led to the establishment of strict regimes which control both the fieldwork and the future of the finds and sites. With their wealth of archaeological sites of every period, Italy, Greece and Turkey each have a more or less centralised archaeological service with responsibility for protection of existing sites, for rescue excavations in advance of both private and public construction and building, and for the maintenance of local and state museums. Other research projects are mounted by local universities, often as part of major collaborative international enterprises. The long history of exploration by 'foreign' scholars has led to the establishment by Britain, as well as many other countries, of institutes to act as bases for research. Each of their projects, however, is subject to rigorous monitoring by the state service.

Each project director will have to demonstrate in an application to the appropriate officials that he or she is qualified to carry out the research, has made proper provision for security of the finds, and has the resources to carry out conservation and publication as well as the fieldwork. The project director is normally expected to have the backing of a university or other institution which can guarantee the completion of the work. In addition, in Greece and Turkey, it is a requirement that a local archaeologist will be appointed as a team member by the state archaeological service to represent the state's interests. In Greece the area of the excavation must be purchased and ownership transferred to the Greek State so that no dispute arises over title to the finds made. In each area finds must be transferred to a local museum or collection for permanent storage.

3.5 Funding for UK-based projects

Once the project design is completed, the director must consider the fundamental issue of fund-raising. Within the academic disciplines of the arts and humanities, archaeology is easily the most expensive form of research. It requires larger teams of researchers and the use of a wider range of equipment and technology than research in, say, the fields of literature or historical studies. The most expensive year, 1996, (including fieldwork and post-excavation work) at Çiftlik cost £20,000, whilst in Greece, where the labour costs are higher, a major season could now cost in the region of £60,000.

There are three principal sources of funding potentially available to project directors.

- Government-funded bodies
- Private trusts, organisations and individuals
- Corporate sponsorship

Whether or not all types of funding are applied for, and in what proportion of the overall budget, will vary from one project to another. However, all project directors will make applications to the government-funded sources of support a first priority.

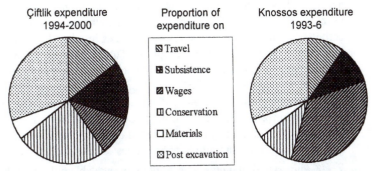

Çiftlik expenditure 1994-2000

Proportion of expenditure on

Knossos expenditure 1993-6

◲ Travel

◪ Subsistence

▨ Wages

▥ Conservation

▢ Materials

▣ Post excavation

Fig 3.2 No two excavations have the same problems or requirements and this is reflected in expenditure under different headings. Getting to Turkey is relatively expensive but subsistence costs there are cheaper than in Greece. While wage costs in Greece are much higher, the construction of a sea wall at Çiftlik was a major budget element. The provision for post-excavation work emphasises its importance, accounting for 30% of the overall expenditure to date at each site.

Government-funded bodies

There are four principal sources of funding for archaeological projects which ultimately derive, fully or partially, from tax-payers' money.

- *The Arts and Humanities Research Board* (AHRB) is a government-funded organisation with the published aims of promoting and supporting excellence in research in the arts and the humanities; to improve the breadth and depth of our knowledge and understanding of human culture, both past and present; to support the development of highly qualified people in the arts and humanities; and to promote and support the dissemination of the results of research in the arts and humanities.

- *The British Academy* is an independent learned society, the national academy for the humanities and social sciences. The Academy represents and promotes the interests of learning and research, nationally and internationally. It also acts as a grant-awarding body, sponsoring its own research projects and facilitating the work of others.

- *The British Academy-sponsored Schools and Institutes abroad.* The Schools and Institutes are autonomous organisations whose mission is to carry out and facilitate academic research and fieldwork overseas; to provide the means of publishing and disseminating the results of that work; and, in some areas, to provide an academic base offering a range of scholarly and logistical support services, including accommodation, library and archive facilities. Archaeology has usually been perceived by most of the institutions as their core activity, but all have a wide spread of interests in other disciplines. The Schools and Institutes comprise: The British Institute of Archaeology at Ankara; The British School at Athens; The British Institute in Eastern Africa; The British School of Archaeology in Iraq; The British Institute of Persian Studies; The British School at Rome; The Council for British Research in the Levant; The Egypt Exploration Society; The Society for Libyan Studies; The Society for South Asian Studies; The Committee for South-east Asian Studies.

- *UK universities and museums.* Funding is available only from the employing institution of a project director through schemes individual to each university and museum.

The application procedure for each of these bodies is based upon a substantial form to be completed by the applicant and shorter forms to be completed by referees. In addition to basic information, such as contact details and qualifications, the bulk of the main application form is focussed upon the project design as explained above. Thus the applicant must outline the research questions, objectives and methods, the fieldwork, post-fieldwork and publication programmes, and the budget.

However, the award of a grant is not the end of the process. All awards are made subject to compliance with a series of terms and conditions. These may include the requirement to report any other awards made or to present copies of publications resulting from the supported research to the funding body. All funding bodies require as a matter of course a full report on the research conducted and may request both an academic and a financial report which should reflect the project design outlined in the application. There may also be attached conditions relating to timing and placing of publications.

Trusts, individual and corporate sponsorships

In addition to the government-funded grant-giving bodies, there are a number of private trusts established by wealthy individuals or families with particular academic interests to support archaeological fieldwork and research. Private academic organisations also make limited funds available to support archaeological research. For example, the Society of Antiquaries of London is charged by its Royal Charter of 1751 with 'the encouragement, advancement and furtherance of the study and knowledge of the antiquities and history of this and other countries'. Two other UK-based organisations that support Classical archaeology are the Society for the Promotion of Hellenic Studies and the Society for the Promotion of Roman Studies. The Leverhulme Trust was established in 1925 under the will of Lord Leverhulme, founder of Lever Brothers – now Unilever plc. Such charitable funding has become increasingly significant in the academic and educational life of the UK.

Another form of potential private funding is via wealthy individuals who might be willing to contribute towards the costs of a project in which they have a personal interest. This may be done as a private, and frequently anonymous donation, or via a 'Friends' organisation. Finally, corporate sponsorship is a relatively rare form of funding for archaeological projects and is only really applicable to projects which can offer an outcome of value to the business concerned.

Chapter 4
Archaeological Prospecting

4.1 Surface survey

> Excavation must be seen as the culmination of the investigation of the site. We should only resort to surgery after intensive pre-operative examination.
>
> (Barker)

The oldest and in some ways the simplest method of detecting archaeological sites is to search for them visually on the ground. Surface survey, or as it is more commonly known, fieldwalking or field survey, is the systematic visual survey of an area in order to record evidence of previous human activity. It can often reveal sites much more easily than excavation and is certainly less expensive. Such survey can be intensive (e.g. survey of a single field in a suspected area of settlement) or extensive (a regional survey) and can involve a variety of strategies depending on the aims and resources of the project. Surveys might be restricted to the recording of certain types of artefact (e.g. pottery or metalwork) or to recording material from restricted periods (e.g. Archaic or late Roman). Fieldwalkers should be familiar with the artefacts which they might find, since otherwise objects could go unnoticed or could be wrongly attributed. To the untrained eye the differences between worked and unworked flint, for example, are very difficult to distinguish. Fieldwalking on agricultural land which has been recently ploughed and then weathered after rain produces the best results. Finds are more easily spotted after rain, especially in diffused light and when vegetation is low, and accordingly from October to March is usually the best time for fieldwalking in Britain. Drier parts of the Classical world have shorter ideal times for surface survey. All areas need to be re-walked at different times of year, and after ploughings to take advantage of changing conditions.

Intensive survey is often organised with the aid of a grid system imposed upon the area (Fig. 4.1). Fieldwalkers walk in lines across the squares of the grid, collecting material in bags for later study, or identifying objects, recording them and leaving them on site. The smaller the

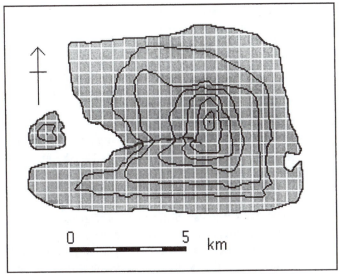

Fig 4.1 Island of Bathos, base grid with contours at 50m. intervals.

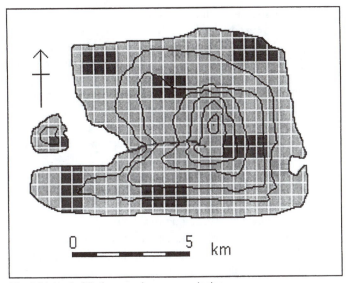

Fig 4.2 Island of Bathos, random survey design.

squares and the larger the team, the more detailed the survey will be. In a simpler technique, lines can be laid out across the area using measuring tapes and ranging poles and one person walks along each line, collecting artefacts from either side. This method is good for rapid reconnaissance but can miss small scatters of material if the lines are too far apart.

When studying very large areas it is not practical to use intensive methods and some sort of sampling of the region is necessary for an **extensive survey**. Where the region is geographically and geologically uniform, random sample sites may be selected from a map (Fig. 4.2). More commonly, study of maps will reveal that a survey has distinct zones determined by varying geographical, environmental and geological conditions. In this case, each of the different zones must be sampled in order to ensure coverage of a wide range of landscapes and environments, each of which might contain different types of archaeological site (Fig. 4.3). Setting up transects – parallel strips across the region, spaced randomly or in a systematic pattern and then intensively fieldwalked – is another technique (Fig. 4.4). It is often appropriate to base the sampling design on already known or suspected sites, using these as a starting point from which to extend the survey. Different survey and sampling methods are frequently combined within the same project, for example intensive fieldwalking over and around a known site such as a Roman villa may be combined with transects across the hinterland, sampling different geographical zones (uplands, hillside, valley, etc.) and environmental contexts (pasture, wetlands, etc).

Typical finds from fieldwalking might include pottery sherds, flint and stone artefacts, coins and charcoal scatters. Single finds might not be significant – they may have been accidentally dropped or brought to the site in refuse or during manuring – but concentrations often provide evidence of human activity and settlement. It is also important to look for scatters of building debris such as brick and tile fragments, pieces of cut stone or deposits of mortar which can indicate where stones have been carried away from destroyed buildings.

Blank areas can be just as important as areas which contain large quantities of artefacts. Absence of artefacts is often an indicator of different land use in antiquity (ancient pasture or woodland, for example, in areas which are now under the plough), although it should always be remembered that some geological and natural occurrences such as flooding rivers, hill-wash, earthquakes and erosion can distort the picture.

Surface survey may also reveal larger ground features and earthworks, especially in woodland where sites cannot be discovered by aerial photography. Fieldwalking may thus lead to the recording of ditches or

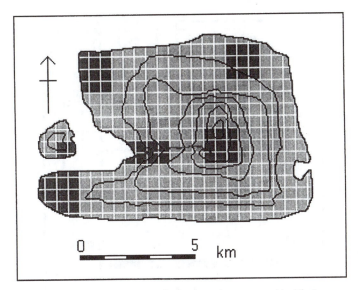

Fig 4.3 Island of Bathos, survey design based on geographical factors.

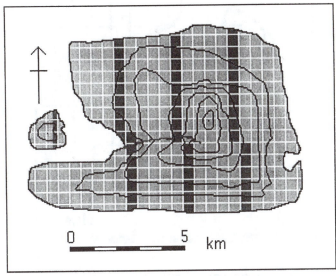

Fig 4.4 Island of Bathos, survey design by systematic transects.

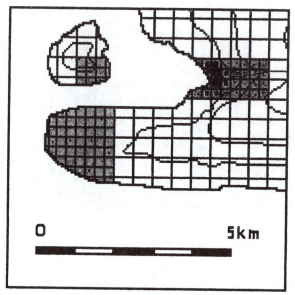

Fig 4.5 Details of geographically based survey on Bathos.
Finds shown as dot density.

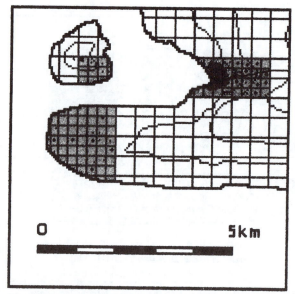

Fig 4.6 Detail of geographically based survey on Bathos.
Find areas shaded.

other defensive features which casual observers had assumed were simply field boundaries or meaningless 'humps and bumps' in the ground.

The results of surface surveys are plotted on maps in a variety of ways (Figs. 4.5 and 4.6), but archaeologists are always concerned to reveal relative densities of different categories of artefacts (i.e. those used for different purposes, whether domestic, agricultural or industrial) and to look for correlations between type and date of artefact assemblages with the different sites which can be located in an area.

4.2 Aerial photography

Photographs of the landscape taken from the air can show sites which are difficult to see on the ground or can make details of known sites more clear (Fig. 4.7). Black and white film is mostly used for its strong contrasts and for economy, though infra-red film can also be very effective, showing up dramatically features which are invisible to the human eye. Vertical views create relatively little distortion of the shapes of such sites and are therefore easy to map. Oblique photographs often produce better images (showing up contours, for example) but they require a special camera. Stereoscopic photographs, where two adjacent, slightly overlapping, images are taken simultaneously, give a three-dimensional effect (thus emphasising relief) when seen through a stereoscopic viewer. All aerial photographs need to be rectified before planning, usually with the help of a computer programme, through a process known as photogrammetry. The patterns on the landscape which can be seen in aerial photographs are created by different circumstances.

Shadow marks occur when the sun is low in the sky and shadows or highlights are thrown into and across earthworks such as ditches, banks and mounds which may contain buried walls. Winter conditions can also produce good results when snow and frost melt more slowly in hollows and therefore show up as white marks on open ground.

Soil marks are produced by different tones of sub-soil revealed by deep ploughing. A ploughed-out chalk bank, for example, would show up as a light mark amidst the darker soil. Soil marks are also created when ploughs hit buried building remains and drag up fragments of mortar or other building material. The very fact that soil marks show up at all proves that the site is in the process of being destroyed.

Crop marks reveal buried features which are affecting the growth of the crop above them. A buried ditch cut through the sub-soil may hold more moisture which would benefit the crop, making it grow taller and ripen later (a positive crop mark). Conversely, a buried wall will restrict access to moisture, resulting in stunted growth, earlier ripening and a different crop colour (a negative crop mark). Infra-red sensitive film can be used to exaggerate slight colour differences, as riper crops reflect more infra-red light. Parch marks are created when grass growing over solid buried features withers during severe drought conditions. Whilst darker

Fig 4.7 Vertical aerial photograph of the Roman site at Wroxeter (ancient Viroconium).

crop marks are usually caused by ditches cut into sub-soil and back-filled with humus-rich soil which holds moisture, it is important to remember that on clay soils ditches may be cut to improve drainage; in which case, even if no drainage pipes are present, the ditches may have been back-filled with gravel or other materials which cause the soil above them to dry out. In wettish conditions such drainage features show as lighter crop marks in aerial photographs – they may be mimicked by archaeological features which are cut into clay sub-soils and back-filled with building materials, thus causing positive features to appear as negative images.

Aerial photography has produced spectacular results, although its effectiveness is limited to certain conditions. Soil marks only show in ploughed fields, for example, and crop marks are best produced on lighter, well-drained soils. Certain crops, like cereals, are more sensitive to moisture variation than others. The effects of these variations may only last a week or two, requiring the same area to be re-flown and re-photographed at intervals for a full picture, and this can be expensive. Aerial photography, like geophysical survey (below), is most effective in areas of arable cultivation with a reasonable depth of soil – conditions which are much more restricted in Italy or Greece than in Britain. The transition from wet to dry soil conditions is also much more rapid in the Mediterranean area, a factor which severely limits the period during which crop marks will show up. Even so, keen observation or good fortune can have spectacular results, as in the case of the Roman field patterns created by *centuriation* – the allocation of regular parcels of land to legionary veterans – which were recorded in military photographs of southern Italy.

The majority of aerial photographs are taken from aeroplanes at a considerable altitude. Balloons and kites have also been used effectively to take aerial photographs, especially when lower-altitude photographs are required. Balloons with radio-controlled cameras are especially useful for taking low-level aerial photographs, either of areas undergoing detailed surface survey or of sites which are being excavated.

Large archives of military and government-planning photographs (mainly verticals used for mapping) are available in some countries, and these are a major source of primary archaeological information which should be consulted even before surface survey is undertaken. Older aerial photographs can be especially valuable since they often show sites which have since been destroyed – and there is a growing number of archives of aerial photographs (mainly oblique views) which have been specifically taken for archaeological purposes. Unfortunately access to archives of aerial photographs can be very limited in some areas and taking photographs from planes is actually prohibited in some countries for reasons of national security.

4.3 Site mapping

Creating plans of archaeological features within a landscape can display information not visible in aerial reconnaissance. Similarly, mapping the surface contours of a site can show subtle undulations in seemingly flat ground. The resulting plans may reveal the remains of banks and ditches, building platforms or roads which have been almost ploughed away.

Surveys of surface contours produce topographic maps which are an essential part of the preparation for excavation, but may also stand alone as a record of the surviving site.

The creation of a contoured area plan or overall topographical site survey of this kind is sufficiently complex to require the help of an experienced surveyor. Already in the seventeenth century the Ordnance Survey in Britain (and similar military agencies in the rest of Europe) had developed surveying techniques using mathematical principles and simple instruments. Measurements were traditionally taken with long metal **chains** of fixed length combined with the use of a **plane table** – a simple device enabling the angles of lines of sight to be transferred to a scaled drawing. The qualifications expected of the Chief Engineer of the Ordnance in 1683 speak for themselves:

> ...to be well skilled in all parts of the Mathematicks, more particularly in Stereometry, Altemetry, and Geodoesia. To take Distances, Heights, Depths, Surveys of Land, Measures of solid Bodies, and to cut any part of ground to a proportion given;...to be perfect in Architecture, civil and military...to draw and design the situation of any place, in their due Prospects, Uprights, and Perspectives;.... To keep perfect draughts of every the Fortifications, Forts, and Fortresses of Our Kingdom, their situation, figure and profile...

The same skills are still very relevant to the field archaeologist and it is no coincidence that many early archaeologists were trained military engineers.

From the late eighteenth century the Ordnance Survey embarked on the mapping of England using the method of triangulation to create large-scale maps. Each region was planned with the aid of a series of measured triangles expanding from an initial base line. The requirements of navigation and of military artillery for accurate instruments had led by this period to the development of the **theodolite**. This is, essentially, a telescope mounted on a tripod which can be rotated vertically and horizontally against finely graduated scales. By this means vertical and horizontal angles can be measured with great accuracy and trigonometry can be used to record the location of any distant but visible point. Accuracy in this kind of surveying, whether of a landscape or an individuate site, is vital since errors in triangulation are cumulative and frequent cross-checks are essential, especially when the site is on a slope. Given the nature of the terrain in which so many of the major Classical

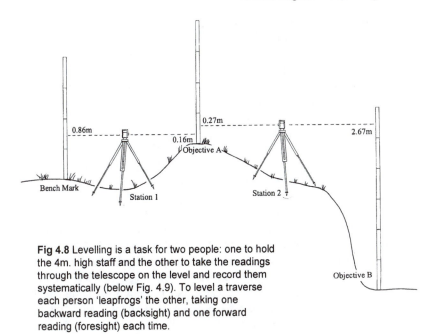

Fig 4.8 Levelling is a task for two people: one to hold the 4m. high staff and the other to take the readings through the telescope on the level and record them systematically (below Fig. 4.9). To level a traverse each person 'leapfrogs' the other, taking one backward reading (backsight) and one forward reading (foresight) each time.

Station (position of level)	Objective (position of staff)		Backsight (previous position)	Height of telescope on level		Foresight (next position)	Real level of objective
1	Bench Mark 10.00m*	+	0.86	10.86			
1	A			10.86	–	0.16	10.70
2	A (10.70)	+	0.27	10.97			
2	B			10.97	–	2.67	8.30
3	B (8.30)	+	2.41	10.71			
3	C			10.71	–	1.16	9.55
4	C (9.55)	+	1.68	11.23			
4	D			11.23	–	2.62	8.61
1	D (8.61)	+	2.26	10.81			

Fig 4.9 Levelling: transcript of surveyor's note book. Traverse around the mound at Assiros, (see Fig. 4.10) completing the circuit by returning to station 1. The result of each addition or subtraction is the starting point for the next calculation. Note the small error to be expected in a traverse of this kind (0.05m.).

*Temporary reference datum until real ASL (above sea level) could be calculated.

sites in Greece, Turkey or the near east are set, it is hardly surprising that detailed topographic plans have only been completed for a few of them.

The theodolite, or the simpler surveyor's **level**, are both used to measure the levels of points in the landscape in relation to a known fixed height in order to complete a contour survey (see Figs. 4.8, 4.9 and 4.10). This fixed height is normally a temporary reference point, or **datum**, located on an immovable object or a peg concreted into the ground, conveniently near to the site. This point can later be tied in with permanent **bench-marks**, official measures of height above sea-level which are scattered around the countryside and marked on government maps.

If necessary, sketch plans can be made with the use of little or no technical equipment. Simple sketch surveys can be produced by pacing out distances from a known point, and perhaps taking compass bearings to assist location, but the accuracy of such plans is very limited. In the absence of a theodolite, measurements of smaller areas can be taken from an arbitrary baseline or from a grid laid out by triangulation or by using a 3:4:5 triangle (see Chapter 6); the important thing is to relate the site baseline to fixed points in the landscape (perhaps a building, field boundary or a road) which can be found on maps and will allow future archaeologists and historians to locate the site accurately.

Archaeology does not, of course, concern itself only with what lies beneath the ground. The survey and measured drawing of standing monuments is a vital part of field research whether in its own right or as a preliminary to excavation. The detail of such recording may range from simple sketches to stone-by-stone drawings of buildings using vertical grids or baselines. Photographs are always taken to support the results of all surveys.

In the past fifteen years the development of the **Electronic Distance Measurement** instrument (EDM, also known as a 'total station' when it is combined in the same machine with a theodolite) has led to great saving in the time and effort required for a field survey. It sends out an infra-red beam which bounces back to the instrument from a reflector (also known as the objective or target) mounted on a staff and the relative distance, height and angle of the point to be measured is calculated automatically (as long as the EDM has been programmed with data about the local temperature and air pressure using the integral key-pad). Thus two people, one at the EDM and one moving the reflector, can record a series of points within a radius of about a kilometre in a relatively short period of time, the readings being automatically logged into the machine electronically for later analysis. Newer total stations include 'intelligent' reflectors where the reflector is attached to a computer, enabling the

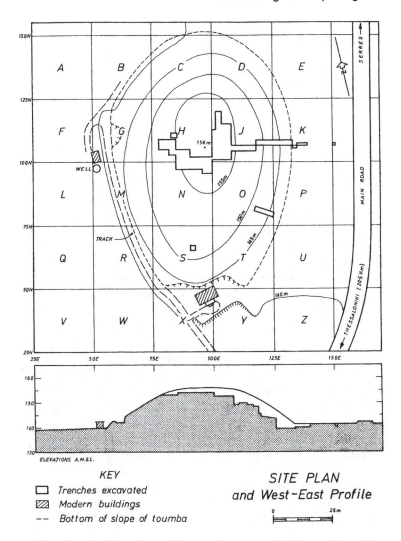

Fig 4.10 Contour plan with initial trench layout – Assiros. The area was divided into major squares 25 x 25m. and the contours at 5m. intervals show the shape of the settlement mound. A combination of trenches and open areas were used to explore the sides and summit.

person who is moving between parts of the site which are being recorded to make notes as the survey proceeds and to see a developing plan on the computer screen. As well as being used to survey the general topography of sites and location of individual trenches on sites which are being excavated, the accuracy of total stations is such that they can be used to provide three-dimensional co-ordinates to the nearest millimetre for individual finds.

The **Global Positioning System** (GPS) uses information from satellites to locate positions on the Earth's surface. The accuracy of such systems is often superb, to less than 1 centimetre in some cases. Surveys can also be completed very quickly which can be cost-effective, but the machines themselves are expensive and access to them may therefore be very limited. Where the landscape is rugged and relatively unmapped, as in parts of Greece and Turkey, GPS systems have considerable potential for the accurate location and survey of large sites.

Information from surveys can be presented as maps at various scales. Data from topographic and planimetric surveys can be combined on the same maps; hatching is often added to indicate more clearly the break of a slope or the shape of a hollow. Data can also be enhanced by computer to produce three-dimensional wire-frame models which exaggerate often very slight contours into a coherent picture of the site topography. With the assistance of **Geographical Information Systems** (GIS) software, complex visualisations of topographical features can be achieved within which it is possible to move from realisations of distant bird's-eye perspective views to discovering, for instance, the three-dimensional co-ordinates of an individual tessera within a Roman pavement. Such graphically interpretable computerised records, preserved as 'soft' copy, are increasingly forming a major aspect of archaeological archives.

4.4 Geophysical survey and soil sampling

Geophysical surveying allows archaeologists to 'see' beneath the ground surface without having to excavate. It can create maps of buried sites already known to be of archaeological interest, suggesting the position of features and therefore allowing excavators to focus their resources on specific areas (see Figs. 4.11 and 4.12).

Once fixed points have been established on the site, usually by imposing a grid system, a number of different techniques can be used. **Resistivity survey** detects the resistance of buried features and sub-soils to the passage through them of an electric current. Damp soil such as that, perhaps, within the fill of a ditch or a pit, will allow the current to pass easily, whereas dry, compacted soil or buried stone (including bedrock) and brick will resist it. Various types of equipment are available for the measurement of resistivity. With the so-called Martin-Clark equipment, four electrodes are inserted in line about fifteen centimetres into the ground and one metre apart. A low electric current is passed between two of the electrodes and the other two pick up the resistance which is measured on a meter connected to them by a cable. Moving these electrodes across a site can be time-consuming and requires two operators and this has led to changes to the configuration of the electrodes, such as the addition of a fifth electrode, which allows four to remain engaged while the first is moved to the front of the line in preparation for the next reading. The most common form of resistivity equipment in use today, however, has two electrodes mounted onto a frame which also carries the meter. The resistance between the two mobile probes is constantly compared with that between two static probes which are ideally set in a nearby location with relatively low resistance, thus ensuring positive readings at the points tested by the mobile probes. This system has greatly speeded up the process, as one operator can walk the instrument across the site taking measurements at every metre or half-metre interval. Moving the fixed probes to reestablish the readings recorded on previous days enables continuity of resistivity surveys over a prolonged period of time.

The results of a resistivity survey are commonly displayed as dot-density plots which reveal areas of high and low resistance. They can be displayed as graphs with peaks and troughs showing high and low resistance. Since the readings are taken in runs across a site the graphs for single runs can be displayed alongside each other, thus producing what is effectively a contoured image. In either case, the 'anomalies' which emerge in the images cannot be confidently identified or dated without excavation (the difference between rubble layers and bedrock may not be apparent, for example), although the forms of some types of site – Roman forts or villas for example – are so well known that an educated guess can be made. Resistivity surveys are particularly well adapted to detecting stone structures and linear features such as roadways, walls and ditches. As with aerial photographs, some soil conditions, particularly where there are underlying chalks, may reverse normal positive and negative effects. Not all soils, however, are conducive to producing good readings: waterlogged or extremely dry soils will severely limit the variations in resistance to electric current. For obvious reasons, it is also necessary to consider likely weather conditions when planning to conduct a resistivity survey, since all readings need to be taken under similar conditions if they are to be comparable.

It is particularly hard to predict results in Mediterranean conditions. For much of the year the soil is very dry, while shallow soils over uneven bedrock – or a great depth of masonry as at Knossos – can present a very confused image. Nevertheless, when resistivity and magnetic (see below) survey techniques are combined important finds have been obtained at a variety of sites. Examples include location of the defensive ditches which mark the boundary of the lower city of Troy; the discovery of the canal cut by the Persian Great King Xerxes so that his fleet would avoid the dangerous headland of Mount Athos in Macedonia; and the plan of the ancient settlement at Lake Stymphalos in the Peloponnese.

Magnetic survey measures variations in the strength of the magnetic field and/or magnetic susceptibility of soil. Topsoil contains randomly occurring magnetic particles, mainly oxides. Solid features such as stone walls contain fewer such particles, whereas pits and ditches, cut into the subsoil and filled to a greater depth with redeposited topsoil, contain more. Buried metals also disturb the random background of particles, as does fired clay, brick and tile. Heat above 700°C (from hearths or kilns for example) causes the particles to align themselves with the magnetic field of the Earth where they become fixed upon cooling. The instruments used to detect such anomalies include the **proton magnetometer** which gives readings of the absolute magnetic field at any one point. The results need to be calibrated, as certain types of natural geology and the proximity of iron structures (e.g. fences, railway lines, and buried or overhead power cables) will affect the results. Easier to use is the **proton gradiometer**: this consists of two liquid-filled bottles set two metres apart on a pole which is held vertically. The magnetic field of a particular point will affect the liquid in the lower bottle more than that in the higher one; this difference is recorded and comparison of a number of such readings will produce measurements of the relative strengths of the field. Often a bleeper is attached to the instrument to give audible signs of strong anomalies. A **differential fluxgate gradiometer** is the most commonly used magnetometer, as it can give continuous readings as the operator walks over the site, thus producing a fuller picture of any buried features. It can also be used to take individual readings like a soil resistivity meter. All magnetic survey results are prone to distortion from modern buried metals and igneous bedrock and, in the case of the proton magnetometer, nearby metal fences and electric cables. Dense vegetation can also limit success. Depending on the interval between readings magnetometry can also reveal much smaller features than resistivity, such as iron objects, post-holes and hearths, and pottery dumps.

Fig 4.11 Wroxeter SE sector: results of geophysical survey showing the grid pattern of the streets and some details of buildings within each insula.

Fig 4.12 Wroxeter: plan of SE sector derived from geophysical data presented in Fig. 4.11.

The diagrams below and opposite (Figs. 4.13 and 4.14) show the plan and section of a hypothetical Roman auxiliary fort. Consider what results would emerge from different prospecting techniques if these were applied to this kind of site. Suggested solution on page 59.

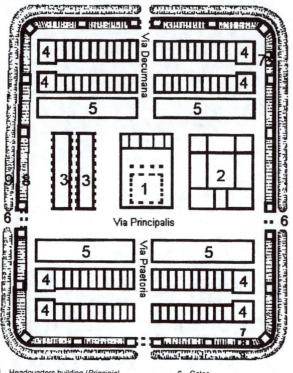

1	Headquarters building (*Principia*)	6	Gates
2	Commanding officer's house (*Praetoria*)	7	Intervallum street (*via sagularis*)
3	Granaries (*horrea*)	8	Rampart
4	Barrack blocks	9	Ditches
5	Stables		

Fig 4.13 Schematic plan of Roman auxiliary cavalry fort.

Computer enhancement can help to sharpen the data resulting from resistivity and magnetometer surveys, sifting out the background 'noise' and emphasising anomalies. Results can be presented as dot-density plans (where concentrations of dots represent anomalies), grey-scale plots (where dots of various sizes produce a graded black and white image) or three-dimensional magnetic contour maps.

Metal detectors (pulse induction meters and soil conductivity meters) are in effect much less sensitive kinds of magnetometer. They can be useful for rapid, shallow surveying or to check spoil-heaps for coins and small metal objects which may have been missed by the excavators. They are, however, too often associated with the destruction of evidence when objects are removed from their archaeological contexts by treasure hunters.

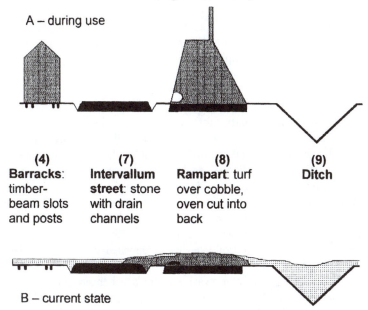

A – during use

(4)	(7)	(8)	(9)
Barracks: timber-beam slots and posts	**Intervallum street**: stone with drain channels	**Rampart**: turf over cobble, oven cut into back	**Ditch**

B – current state

Fig 4.14 Schematic section across a Roman auxiliary cavalry fort.

Ground-penetrating radar is a technique which sends pulses of radiowaves into the ground: these are reflected by the different levels and features up to eight metres below the surface. The time taken for the pulse to return to the detector is measured, enabling a three-dimensional picture of buried features to be constructed. This works very successfully on well-drained, sandy soils, and even to 'see through' concrete surfaces. The equipment is, however, so expensive that it is beyond the reach of many excavators unless there is funding to hire specialist operators with their own equipment.

Taking samples of the soil can reveal a great deal about the nature of a site without having to excavate on a large scale. **Probes**, long solid metal rods with a T-bar handle, are driven into the ground until they meet resistance from buried features: the lines of walls may, for example, be planned using this method. **Augers** are similar tools, but with hollow, cork-screw ends, and are designed to bring samples of buried deposits to the surface. Both of these techniques must be used with great care, as they are destructive by their very nature and can damage small or fragile buried features. **Phosphate analysis** can reveal areas of occupation by measuring the amount of phosphorus in the soil. Phosphates are absorbed naturally by humans and animals and then deposited in excreta. It is also traceable in soil where bone has decayed away. These phosphates become fixed in the soil (in a way that modern agricultural phosphate fertilisers do not) and samples can be taken from the surface of ploughed fields or by auger for analysis in the laboratory. The mapping of any concentrations of phosphorus may reveal areas of human burial, occupation or animal stock-keeping.

Magnetic susceptibility survey can take place in the field or in the laboratory. Sensors can show variations in the density of the magnetic particles across a site in the topsoil itself (rather than in features, as seen in magnetic survey). High densities may indicate areas where burning has taken place or where organic manuring or the dumping of rubbish (which often contains small fragments of charcoal or fired material) has occurred, revealing human occupation and land use in places where no other detectable remains survive. Care must be taken in interpreting such results, however, as topsoils can be redeposited by erosion or land reclamation.

As has been seen, all non-invasive methods of archaeological prospection have their limitations. The best and safest results are achieved when, as in the case of the Wroxeter Hinterland Project, a variety of geophysical and survey techniques are employed. Figures 4.13 and 4.14 show possible results from a variety of different approaches, and it can be seen that only the application of several techniques would make a reasonably full picture of buried features possible.

Possible results of different prospection techniques used on a Roman Fort.

Aerial Photography:

Shadow marks: rampart and ditch would show in raking sunlight.

Soil marks: Ploughing has exposed the top of the surviving rampart and might eventually drag up material from the road surface.

Crop marks: very poor growth over the street, sub-normal growth over the rampart and strong growth over the ditch; very unlikely that the barrack block would show up. Oven would be invisible in any aerial photograph.

Geophysical survey:

Resistivity survey: road and rampart both likely to be detected as high resistance anomalies; low resistance over ditch is likely.
Barracks and oven unlikely to be detected.

Magnetometer survey: oven would show as a 'hot' spot due to fired clay lining. Ditch would be next strongest anomaly; street and rampart also probably detectable as low readings.
Barracks unlikely to be detected.

Chapter 5
Excavation

5.1 Excavation strategy

As we have seen, excavations are destructive events, the ultimate in experiments because they cannot be repeated. Decisions to excavate must therefore not to be taken lightly, and when they are taken this must be done with full knowledge of as much contextual information as possible. The archaeologist who is contemplating subjecting a site to the excavation process must be able to answer 'yes' to all the following questions:

- Do the likely results justify the damage to the site that will be caused by excavation?

- Is this the best site available to answer my research question?

- Do I have sufficient resources (human and financial) to see the project through to conservation, presentation and publication?

- Having considered all alternatives, do I still think that this excavation is the only way forward archaeologically?

The broad issues relating to project planning have been considered in Chapter 3, but before proceeding to give an account of the practical methods used by excavators, it is worth looking at the different types of site which are likely to confront them, since consideration of the nature of the site to be excavated will help to decide the methods to be used. Initial factors which affect the approach to excavation are whether the site is urban or rural, an open field or a site where a building has been standing.

It is in the nature of **urban sites** that they tend to display the evidence of long periods of occupation with sequences of building and re-building, including laying and repairing of services. This can cause profound challenges for stratigraphic interpretation since relatively modern features like electricity cables may be far deeper in the soil than the much more ancient levels through which they have been cut. Whilst it may be attractive to call in the bulldozers to remove very recent levels on an urban site, great care has to be taken not to disturb islands of ancient material round which modern features have been cut deeply. The stratigraphic deposits of urban sites are rarely simple, with horizontal levels deposited conveniently in succession. Features such as brick-lined Victorian cellars often prove to have cut through and destroyed many layers of vital earlier evidence. Where cellars occur there is usually little alternative to emptying them of their contents, even though this inevitably leaves large holes in the site which can be very unsightly in photographs. The only benefits of the existence of cellars are that once emptied of their fills they may offer a preview of the stratigraphy, and the opportunity to conduct 'key-hole' excavations into even deeper levels in order to evaluate the archaeological potential of the site.

Multi-period urban sites cause other headaches for archaeologists, since however stable the upper layers may be – and there is nothing more disheartening than finding buried concrete features which need to be removed, noisily and expensively, with pneumatic drills – there is no guarantee whatsoever that there will be stable levels beneath them. The urban archaeologist therefore has to be continually aware of safety hazards, and shoring-up of trenches after about 1.5 metres is normal practice. Even so, it is extremely common to find loose deposits, or even voids, underneath substantial more recently built features, and the director of an excavation may have to abandon parts of the site because it is simply unsafe to continue to work in them. Further difficulties are caused by power cables, gas pipes and sewers, all of which are potentially highly dangerous: prudent archaeologists consult the records of service providers, but also never fail to bear in mind that these records are, more often than not, incomplete. Such considerations commonly render it difficult to see excavation plans through as they were originally designed. It is only the bold (or reckless) director who persists in continuing to excavate underneath power cables which are still live, though occasionally such decisions are made if the threat to a rescue dig is so serious and so immediate that the only alternative is abandoning the site. The excavation of part of the Basilica of St Polyeuktos in Istanbul (Constantinople) had to be completed under the city's main power cable in order to complete recording before an underpass was bulldozed through the east end of the building. On that occasion the authorities agreed to switch off the electricity supply to a large part of the city temporarily in order to insert extra insulation and physical support round the exposed sagging section of cable.

It is somewhat more likely, but by no means certain, that the stratigraphic analysis of **rural sites** which are under pasture or cultivation may be simpler, since there is a higher possibility of finding one-period sites, or at least that multi-period sites will be much less disturbed by service trenches. Even so, drainage of clay soils may have been effected by deeply-cut pipe trenches, and old tree-holes can be very difficult to define because they have uncertain ragged edges, especially if stumps have been pulled forcibly from the ground, whilst sideways extending roots have been left to rot in place. Excavators of rural sites, especially in less developed countries also have to take account of considerations of access to the site and availability of water. If there has to be a substantial investment in transport costs, importing basic materials and even in building a dig-house, then practical considerations may militate against selecting the least disturbed rural example of a certain type of site rather than its more accessible but often disturbed and redeveloped urban equivalent. Another consideration when selecting a site may be the extent to which it has been burrowed by different animals. At Assiros the friable soil of the upper levels had proved ideal for mole-rats and badgers who had conducted their own unsystematic excavations while, at the site of a third century BC Macedonian tomb not far away, work was abandoned when it was discovered that the foxes who had their dens in the side of the mound had departed in a hurry leaving behind legions of starving fleas.

Whilst rural sites are generally less fraught with hazards like major power supplies or sewer gases, they can throw up challenges of their own. Thus the excavations at Çiftlik suffered a short delay when the local farmer decided that the carefully measured-in survey pegs would be ideal posts on which to tether his cows! When the cows pulled these pegs from the ground this resulted not only in the temporary loss of the base-survey grid but also caused problems: the cows trailed ropes and pegs into an area where geophysical survey was in progress thus getting themselves and their ropes entangled with the knicker elastic stretched out to mark gridded squares for the soil resistivity survey.

5.2 Trenches

Once a site has been chosen for an excavation, a decision has to be made about the kind or kinds of **trench** to be opened. Archaeological trenches come in all manner of shapes and sizes. The straight, long, thin trench – the 'slit trench' – is the dominant popular image. That such trenches are thought of by the public as normal is probably a result of military associa- tions, recollecting the trenches dug in the First World War. Although such trenches are still dug by archaeologists, modern ones are normally much wider and more open, and the shape of the trench is essentially determined by consideration of function and purpose. Narrow trenches preserve masses of stratigraphic information in their exposed **vertical** sections (Chapter 6.5). In situations where there is a perceived need to understand chronological *sequences*, it may be necessary to keep as many sections as possible on a site. This kind of imperative often applies when excavation is undertaken in parts of the Classical world where, for instance, full pottery sequences have not yet been established and there is a vital need to secure stable frameworks revealing the relative chronologies within and between sites (Chapter 7.4). Where, however, as is the case in much of northern Europe, Italy and Greece, pottery sequences are well understood, the emphasis in excavation may be much more on understanding *structures*. In these cases, it is the **horizontal** dimension which really matters, since failure to expose and record parts of a structure could result in partial understanding and subsequent misinterpretation.

Tiny **keyhole trenches**, also known as test pits or exploratory trenches and often no more than a metre square, are employed in the early stages of evaluation of sites when archaeologists are concerned to discover the depth of overburden (topsoil), the nature of the substrata, or the location of buried features whose presence has been suggested by loose surface finds. Small exploratory trenches are particularly useful where, perhaps because of water-logged conditions or the presence of power cables, geophysical prospecting has been unproductive.

Slit trenches (Fig. 5.1) which can cut across linear features and reveal their relative locations are still useful, especially for revealing fortification systems. Thus it may be appropriate to put slit trenches across the defences of a Roman fort whose broad outline has been determined from visible surface contours or from aerial photographs. The vertical sections provide diagnostic evidence for the shape of ditches, the methods of construction of ramparts and the relative location of internal structures, especially when, as is commonly the case with Roman forts, there is reason to believe that the overall plan of the site will follow reasonably predictable lines. Slit trenches are also extremely useful for determining stratigraphic relationships on the sides of multi-period mounds where total excavation would result in the disappearance of the monument, and narrow trenches cut in the centre of the mound would be impossible for safety reasons.

Before the regular use of earth-moving machinery in archaeological excavations, when hand-digging was inevitable, a combination of keyhole with slit trenches was often used to enable study of large sites. This approach was adopted by Sir Ian Richmond for his research on the Flavian Roman military sites of central Scotland. Using these simple and economical methods he was able to produce plans of the legionary fortress at Inchtuthil and the auxiliary fortress at Fendoch, which

Fig 5.1 W. Dörpfeld excavated widely in Lefkas, between 1900 and 1912, in the belief that it was the Homeric Ithaka. He used deep slit trenches to test for prehistoric levels.

Fig 5.2 Box trenches.

have become influential landmarks in the study of Roman military architecture (see *Roman Britain* by Hill and Ireland, also in this series). Nowadays, however, keyholes and slit trenches are rarely used except in the particular situations detailed above, because their use inevitably entails a significant risk of completely missing important features.

The next stage forward from the use of slit trenches with keyholes was the development by Sir Mortimer Wheeler of the **box system** (or grid

Fig 5.3 Open area excavation at Shepton Mallet with machine stripping in background.

system) of excavation. Following this method the site is marked out with grid lines defining a chequerboard pattern, and square trenches are cut into each square leaving narrow up-standing unexcavated strips, 'baulks', between the excavated square trenches. The baulks are vital to this approach since they preserve the stratigraphic evidence and are also utterly necessary for practical purposes. As it is impossible to locate spoil-heaps next to boxes excavated at the centre of the grid, spoil must be taken away in wheelbarrows on plank runs along the tops of the baulks.

The box system represented a move away from the sampling and partial planning, which was a necessary consequence of digging in slit trenches, towards a process which enabled fuller planning and exploration of buried structures. Near the end of an excavation which follows the box system methodology it may be possible to start removing the baulks, thus completing horizontal exposure, but this process means that a large proportion of the site has to be excavated out of sequence.

Box system excavations are now relatively unusual in Britain. This is in part a reaction to practicalities, since, especially after overnight rain, too many baulks fell down under the strain of repeated wheelbarrow movements. These collapses were doubly disastrous, because they led to injuries to diggers and damage to exposed surfaces. Removing spoil from the centre of extensive box excavations was tedious since wheelbarrows could not pass each other on the narrow baulks. Modern health and safety requirements demand that baulks should be as much as two metres wide and no more than 1.5m. high. In horizontal terms this has the consequence that if a site is divided into boxes, each 10m. square, then 36 sq.m. in every box (i.e. more than one third of the total area) has to be occupied by baulks, and there are serious limitations on the depth to which excavation can be undertaken.

In Greece, however, the box method has been widely applied recently in rescue excavations in advance of road development where sites as much as a kilometre in length have required investigation, and the box trenches have enabled systematic sampling of the site and extensions where necessary without creating spoil removal problems (Fig. 5.2).

By the 1960s **area stripping** was becoming popular. One of the first sites where this was regularly exploited was Wroxeter where it proved particularly effective in locating the Saxon timber-framed buildings which overlay the heart of the Roman city. The traces were so slight that box excavation would probably never have revealed enough features at the same time for their plan to have been recognised, let alone understood. Open excavation is now the favoured approach in many archaeological situations. It allows the removal of contexts layer by layer in sequence across a whole site, and facilitates planning, photography and on-site interpretation. Area stripping represents the completion of the shift from the vertical to the horizontal emphasis in excavation. As such it places a considerable onus on the excavator to be meticulous about recording stratigraphic relationships on paper through notes and drawings as they are revealed, since except at the edges of the trench the vertical relationships cannot be recorded by photography. The lack of an extensive set of photographs of vertical sections is usually more than compensated for in open excavations both by the opportunity to take complete sets of intelligible photographs of exposed structures and by the knowledge that important features will not have been missed as a result of the placing of unexcavated baulks.

Area excavation remains less frequent on deep Mediterranean sites where deposits of 3-8m. are not uncommon and the priorities are often the establishment of a total sequence rather than the excavation of the latest levels of habitation.

A final mention is needed of **step** trenches which are used for deep soundings. Step trenches are employed for the excavation of very deep deposits where shoring of vertical sections is not a practical proposition. In such circumstances, which may apply to mounds or sites which have been subject to regular deposition of hill-wash material, a large, open, initial trench is cut and, as the trench becomes deeper, steps are made which create stable sections whilst reducing the area under excavation. This process enables a vertical record to be maintained which is likely to be vitally important in a deep multi-period site, and eases the removal of soil from the deeper levels since the steps can support barrow runs or ease the process of lifting out buckets of spoil. The system has the consequence that it may only be possible to uncover a relatively small area at the bottom of the trench.

Many modern excavations will involve the digging of a variety of types of trench (Fig. 4.10). Thus area stripping over the central buildings of a Roman fort may well be combined with slit trenches cut across the defence systems where total excavation would not represent a sensible use of available time and money.

5.3 Levels of recovery

The principles of archaeological stratigraphy are discussed in Chapter 7.1. The task of the field archaeologist is to lay bare deposits, layer by layer, and to recognise differences between these deposits which reveal previous activity on the site (e.g. changes in the colour or consistency of the soil). If no such changes are seen after removing one layer, then another arbitrary layer – or spit – can be removed. Any new deposit, however, must be given a new designation in the site records and therefore becomes a new stratigraphic unit or **context** (see Chapter 6.2). A context may be natural (wash from an eroding hillside, perhaps, which may still contain artefacts) or a man-made feature. Once a context has been identified, the archaeologist must then define its full extent in order to understand its relationship to other deposits and to work out a stratigraphic sequence. More obvious man-made contexts include walls, ditches, post-holes and pits: these are often called **features**, but they are contexts nonetheless and should be numbered as such. The principle of 'last in, first out' dictates that the latest contexts within the site should be removed first. Thus the fill of a pit cut through a floor surface, for example, should be removed as a separate context and taken out before the floor itself is excavated. During excavation of the pit it may be appropriate to investigate the layers within its fill by cutting a section through it in order to see the sequence of vertical deposition.

It is therefore clear that, unlike the remote methods of investigating archaeological sites which were discussed in section 5.1, excavation is a destructive technique. As such – and this cannot be over emphasised – an excavation is an unrepeatable experiment and it is therefore vital that as much evidence as possible is revealed, recorded and preserved for future generations of archaeologists to study. Nevertheless, the practicalities of modern excavation, where a lack of resources and time is the norm, force directors into difficult decisions concerning the precision with which the digging is to be carried out.

Sites may be excavated using different levels of recovery, depending on the nature of the evidence and the time and resources available to the project. In order not to disturb important archaeological deposits, some trial trenching is usually required to establish the depth of the overburden. It may then be decided that stripping the upper layers using an earth-moving machine would save a great deal of time and effort. The swift removal by machine of ploughed topsoil in rural contexts, or modern disturbance and construction layers in an urban situation, usually saves much time and therefore represents prudent management of an archaeological project. Even so, if a machine is to be used, a close eye must be kept on its progress by an archaeologist who can order the driver (preferably one with previous experience of archaeological machining) to stop digging immediately if finds or features are revealed. The resulting machine-cut trench will need to be tidied up by hand, cutting sections and removing compacted soil left by the machine in the bottom of the trench. Unless and until the machine-cut trench is thoroughly cleaned in this way, it must be regarded as archaeologically contaminated, since modern materials may have been pushed into much earlier deposits.

The use of machinery to cut through the most recent deposits on an archaeological site is not, however, always appropriate. In some circumstances the conditions of the excavation permit may preclude the use of such machinery (in order to ensure preservation of finds) or the funds may not be available for machine hire. Occasionally the ground may be so soft that heavy machinery must inevitably cause irreparable damage to underlying contexts. In countries which were once the eastern provinces of the Roman empire the cost of machinery may be substantially higher than that of hiring a human workforce, and there are also many places to which it is impossible to deliver the machines. Such practical considerations may well drive the decision to excavate at one site rather than another of the same type and period. Often, therefore, as at Çiftlik, a site will have to be excavated entirely by hand.

Once the area or trenches have been marked out, picks and shovels are used to remove the topmost layer. The director has to pay special attention to the siting of spoil heaps in order to avoid the expense of moving them as the excavation proceeds. Spoil from the excavation must be removed by bucket or wheelbarrow and dumped in a convenient place – preferably not where the trench may have to be extended later and at least a metre from the trench edge in order to facilitate access to the site and to enable the taking of neat photographs. If there is a prevailing wind then it is wise, if possible, to place the spoil heap downwind of the excavation to avoid dust constantly blowing onto newly trowelled surfaces. The location of the spoil heap is always problematic – Murphy's law naturally determines that the most interesting features continue underneath the spoil heap. Indeed Sir Arthur Evans in his first season of excavation at Knossos started by digging test trenches around the perimeter of the palace mound in order to find suitable sites for spoil disposal.

After the removal of each layer, the surfaces of the underlying deposits are cleaned, skimmed with a spade or hand-pick, or scraped with a trowel (a skilled art which takes much practice if it is to be done effectively and sensitively). At this level of recovery, hand shovels are used to transfer the spoil to buckets before removal to the spoil heap or for sieving or sampling. It is vital to keep the site as free of loose spoil as possible in order to see features quickly and clearly. Brushes may be used to clean very dry surfaces or stonework, but otherwise should be avoided as they smear the soil and the edges of contexts can be lost. Very fine tools such as dental picks and toothbrushes are employed for specific, delicate excavation jobs such as skeletons (see Fig. 5.4).

The colour and texture of the soil will vary according to the local conditions – damp soils in British conditions have more colour than dry soils in strong sunlight, whereas the dry soils of the Mediterranean may have more characteristic differences in texture. Thus in the one region the visual clues are more helpful and in the other the feel of the soil under the pick or other tool. Experienced diggers will also often note differences in the sounds made when a spade or trowel hits soils with different textures. For these reasons it is even more important in Greece or Turkey for the excavator or supervisor to take some part in the actual digging: texture can only be felt, not adequately described, even where there are no language barriers.

It is obvious that the more precise the tools used for excavation, the more likely it is that all the archaeological data will be recovered but also that more time will be required to employ them. The same principle can be applied to recording (Chapter 6.7). Although it is clearly preferable to record carefully each potsherd found in a trench, the vast quantities of material found on some Roman sites, for example, would require commitment of inordinate amounts of time and labour which might well be better employed on another aspect of the excavation project. A large dump of sherds from storage vessels like amphorae or pithoi is unlikely to reveal more archaeological information even if it is removed and recorded piece by piece. Project directors must decide which methods are the most appropriate to use, considering the nature of the deposits being excavated and the requirements of the research design.

Fig 5.4 Archaeologists' tools as used in the eastern Mediteranean. The straw basket has now been replaced by the modern version made from rubber tyres. Its name *zembile* is of Arabic origin.

5.4 Unusual environments

Materials decay due to a combination of biological and chemical factors. Micro-organisms attack organic substances. Soils which are extremely acidic or alkaline can have very destructive effects on buried objects. Bone, for example, is unlikely to survive long in very acidic soils. The presence of oxygen and moisture are vital factors in the process of decay, but if these are absent from the archaeological context, as is often the case, for instance, in Egyptian sites, preservation of remains can be impressive.

Extremes of **environmental conditions** can have a marked effect on such preservation. Excessive cold can freeze organic materials such as wood, textiles and soft body tissue, leading to excellent preservation. Such conditions also create great difficulties for excavators, however, since frozen remains may need to be partially thawed on site to allow investigation, but once exposed to the air the fragile material quickly degrades. Usually the removal of such materials from their frozen matrix is better done in a laboratory. An extremely arid environment, such as occurs in desert conditions, also provides excellent desiccating conditions for the survival of organic remains.

Waterlogged sites provide the **anaerobic** conditions – where little or no oxygen is present – wherein metal, timber, textiles, leather and plant remains often survive very well. Thus peat bogs have famously produced some remarkably preserved ancient human bodies. More commonly, wooden structures can often survive in anaerobic conditions, still in their original position. Such remains are usually very fragile and great care must be taken not to damage them. Excavators may install plank walkways above the site from which to work. Metal excavation tools will damage the preserved wood and so wooden or plastic spatulas are often employed, together with water sprays to wash away encrusted mud or peat and to keep the materials from drying out.

Underwater archaeological sites are excavated in accordance with the same general principles and methods as land-based ones. However, the limitations of the time which can be spent under water by a diver (which decreases according to the depth of the site being investigated), and the difficult conditions (including cold and limited movement and visibility) enforce restrictions which preclude some of the techniques of land excavation. Underwater archaeologists, however, do have the advantage that they can float above the surfaces they are working on and thus clean them without having to walk on cleared surfaces. Most prospecting techniques are not effective under water, although magnetometers can be used and sonar imaging and sideways-scanning radar are valuable for locating sites, such as shipwrecks, on the seabed. Once sites are located grids are laid out using tapes, ranging rods and line, and surveying is conducted in essentially the same manner as on land sites.

Sediments can be removed by hand or by use of a compressed air lift (which operates rather like vacuum cleaners). Heavy objects can be removed using inflatable airbags. Measured drawings can be made, as usual, with pencil on plastic film. Often photogrammetry is a more time- and cost-effective technique – vertical photographs are taken of the site (again these are more easily achieved by floating divers than on land sites) from which the drawings are made later. GPS (Chapter 4.3) has also been used effectively to map such sites.

5.5 Digging different materials

Archaeologists may loosely use the word **soil** to refer to many different types of deposit, from clays to silts, sand, gravel and fine wind-blown loess. Similarly the general term 'topsoil' is often given to the upper layers which are likely to have experienced the most disturbance (perhaps through agriculture) and 'natural' to the undisturbed subsoil, which can often be distinguished by dramatic changes of colour caused by the leaching effect of ground-water and lack of humus. Terms like topsoil and subsoil might be handy names on site, but care must be taken not to pre-define layers as non-archaeological and therefore limit their investigation. Some features may well show in the 'topsoil' and will be lost if the latter is machined off. Similarly some 'natural' levels (such as flood-deposited river gravels or hill-wash) may have been redeposited over the archaeological material, and leached out subsoil can still contain artefacts. Further confusion is possible where thin lenses of leached silt from flooding have been deposited over, and thus have hidden, rich occupation layers.

Some soil types are more difficult to work in than others. Sites which are mainly composed of stones and rubble require very careful cleaning if structures are to be discerned from the background material (the matrix). Heavy clays can be physically demanding to dig and their tendency to smear means that maintaining a clean surface in which to spot context changes can be tricky. Rather than trowel such surfaces, peeling back spits of clayey soil along naturally occurring lines of deposition can be effective – in these situations the spade is literally mightier than the trowel.

Sandy sites are problematic due to the difficulty of digging stable trenches, and wooden shuttering to support the trench edges will be necessary to ensure site safety even in relatively shallow trenches. Colour changes in sands are vital archaeological clues, so it is particularly important to locate spoil heaps to ensure that the minimum amount of dust blows back into trenches.

Isolating features by colour change can be relatively simple when, for example, you are dealing with pits cut into chalk, but some fills look remarkably similar to the material into which they are cut. Features like drainage channels and burial pits which have been back-filled immediately after they were dug out with the spoil thrown up by digging them can be especially challenging to define, as can redeposited natural soils. Spotting such changes can sometimes be made easier by spraying the surface with water. This method is often effective with **mud-brick** structures: a mud-brick wall, buried within a matrix of the same mud from which the bricks were originally made, can be difficult to spot, but careful spraying can show the divisions between the individual bricks. The local climate will also play an important part in understanding the features excavated: in Greece a freshly excavated surface with visible pits or other features may well have dried out to an even colour within half an hour.

Unless subjected to extreme environmental conditions, as discussed above (Section 5.4), or carbonised by fire, **timber** structures will usually only survive as marks in the soil. In post-holes, for example, the rotted timber itself may have left a stain in the soil which is noticeably different to the surrounding post-pit (which may also contain packing material). Different construction methods of timber buildings will leave traces other than post-holes. The use of smaller but more frequent uprights will produce a series of shallow stake-holes with pointed bottoms and no packing material. Timber-framed buildings, where the structure sat on the original ground surface, will leave marks only where stones and objects respect the lines of the vanished timbers, which may also have compacted the soil beneath them.

The recovery of **skeletal material** from archaeological sites presents particular problems for field archaeologists. The excavation and extraction of skeletons can be an extremely delicate and therefore very time-consuming task. The rewards as far as bringing the past to life can be extraordinary, but the pressures of project economics require the excavation team to be well prepared, especially in terms of on-site conservation.

The edges of a grave-cut are often the first indication of a burial. The preservation of bone within such a burial, however, varies greatly. Very acidic or alkaline soils may leave no visible traces of the body, since they tend to dissolve bone entirely. Such conditions may also have removed visible evidence of other organic materials such as coffins or grave goods, although the collection of soil samples from the grave may enable reconstruction of these through chemical residues (see Chapter 7.3). Dissolved bone may leave discolouration in the soil, and such shadow traces can be consolidated using a PVA (polyvinylacetate) compound, producing three-dimensional silhouettes, but this is another very time-consuming technique.

When skeletal material is found, excavation tools will switch from trowels/hand-picks to more delicate instruments such as wooden spatulas, dental picks and small artists' brushes or even airbrushes. The availability of a detailed skeleton guide (Fig. 5.5) will enable the less experienced excavator to locate and identify each bone more readily. Once the skeleton has been laid bare, recording can proceed through plans and photographs (Chapter 6.4) and the removal of the bone from its matrix can begin. Each group of bones can be placed in cloth bags and labelled separately for temporary storage (if plastic bags are used they should not be sealed in order to avoid sweating): this will make later reconstruction of the skeleton easier. Bone will inevitably begin to deteriorate once in contact with the air and this may seriously limit its value for later analysis. So the stabilisation of delicate skeletal material as excavation proceeds is vital. (See *First aid for finds*, Chapter 6.6.)

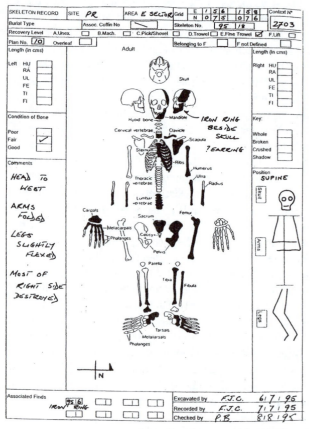

Birmingham University Field Archaeology Unit Tel: 0121 414 5513

Fig 5.5 A skeleton recording guide enables beginners to locate and record even poorly preserved burials.

The expert excavation and recording of burial sites can provide researchers with a wealth of material for analysis of such factors as sex, health, diet, life expectancy, common illnesses and relative wealth and status within populations, burial customs and cultural change.

Chapter 6
Recording the site and the finds

6.1 First principles

Excavations and surveys are only as good as their records. However well the archaeologist has understood the site and however carefully it has been surveyed or excavated, the effort and resources will have been wasted without good diaries, record sheets, plans and sections of the site, together with a detailed and illustrated index to the finds made. Without these records no study or analysis can follow. In the past, far too much information was lost because it was simply entrusted to the excavator's memory, or to brief notebooks. Museums are full of objects from excavations which have lost most of their significance because it is no longer possible to put them in context – we cannot identify their find spots or the other objects with which they were found. A good site record and a good finds record are prerequisites to modern excavation: without them no archaeological work can claim to be scientific.

Ideally, every archaeologist would keep records in exactly the same way so that one site or set of finds could be readily compared with another. In reality, three sets of factors intervene to prevent such a logical outcome.

Firstly, every site is different and has its own characteristics and problems; all too often a system which works well in one place is less practical in another. The contrast between the Mediterranean and Britain can most readily be seen in the quantities of finds made. On many excavations in this country sherds of pottery are so rare that the location of each is recorded in detail. In Greece or Turkey, finds can be so common that the pottery is collected by the basketful from a small area.

Secondly, the nature of an excavation – research or rescue – has an impact. In research excavation, record-keeping is at least as high a priority as excavation: in rescue work, where the timescale is not in the archaeologist's control, the level of record-keeping may well be more selective. Experience alone can guide the archaeologist when it comes to distinguishing between the essential on the one hand, and the desirable but dispensable on the other.

Finally, all archaeologists have their individual experience and inclinations. However desirable uniformity may be, directors and project teams will have their own views on what works best. There are indeed many ways of reaching the same goal. Ultimately what is important is that certain kinds of information are recorded rather than that the information should be recorded in a prescribed way.

In the sections that follow, we have described the categories of record-keeping and examples of the ways we have chosen to implement these in our own fieldwork, rather than to be prescriptive about the way each must be carried out. The most important point is that a recording system appropriate to the site and the conditions of excavation should be thought through before any excavation starts and that every team member, whether working on site or with the finds, should understand the principles in use from their first day as part of the team. In order to ensure that consistency is maintained and that no important information is omitted, it is normal to use pre-printed recording sheets or forms for most tasks. Many of these are now designed so that the data can be readily transferred to a digitally based archive, while some excavators have begun to use laptop computers on site to create the record digitally from the beginning.

One of the first principles that must be taught and observed is that recording has a higher priority than excavation. The record must be made while the evidence still exists. If other tasks cannot be found, the workforce must stand idle while the plans or photographs are made or the details described. The record must also be made in front of the evidence. All too often one hears of excavation directors and their assistants taking pride in their diligence in working late into the evening 'writing up the diary'. This is, however, no more acceptable than it would be for a pathologist to describe the characteristics of blood samples after leaving the laboratory, or for a bank clerk to write down the record of the day's transactions from memory at the end of the day. The archaeologist's memory is no less fallible, even if the outcome of misremembering has less impact on our daily lives. The evening may well be the time for fruitful reflection on the day's work or the discussion of alternative interpretations of the finds and features uncovered, but the record of those finds and features must already exist.

As will be seen in the next chapter, a large part of the work of archaeologists lies in interpreting the data recorded in order to understand the discoveries they have made and to make them intelligible. Interpretation inevitably brings with it a loss of objectivity, and one of the theoretical debates which currently enlivens archaeology is about the extent to which recording on site can, or should, be purely *objective*. In practice, recording is almost meaningless unless what is being recorded is understood – which means interpreting the nature of the cuts and the soils of different texture found within them, or identifying particular items of pottery as belonging to a specific century. The following simple examples (Fig. 6.1) should serve to make this difference clear:

Description in notebook	Interpretation
Two courses of limestone blocks extending for 2.5m.	A wall
A v-shaped cutting into the subsoil, filled with successive layers of water-washed silt and gravel.	A defensive ditch
Mould-made pottery sherds of fine quality with a high gloss red surface.	'Samian' style Roman pottery
Loop of bronze(?) wire found beside the skull of skeleton no. 5.	A bronze earring
A rectangular stone platform with circular dressed stone blocks set around its edge.	A temple foundation

Fig 6.1 The objective record and subjective interpretation are illustrated by these relatively simple examples.

Even though some of these descriptions and interpretations may seem painfully obvious, to avoid premature interpretation it is necessary when recording to employ neutral words such as 'feature', 'object' or 'deposit'.

6.2 The context-based record

The earliest excavators used a diary to keep records of the progress of excavations and finds made. As work progressed, major features such as **levels** or **strata** were distinguished in terms of the vertical relationships between buildings or objects discovered, and finds were located by reference at first to parts of buildings discovered and later to 'trenches' or areas in which they were made – whether these were actual pits or trenches or notional divisions of the site into logical units of, say, 5m. × 5m. All finds were (and usually still are) located by reference to area, level and date of discovery so that the diary formed the index to the work as a whole. Today the diary is seen more as the *interpretative* record, detailing progress, discussing different possibilities, and providing a regular overview of the significance of each part of the excavation in the understanding of the whole.

As the practices of excavation and recording became more refined – and the teamwork involved in the study and publication of the discoveries grew more important – a more flexible system became vital, both to cope with large amounts of information of different kinds and to avoid confusion. Formerly, it was usual for each area supervisor to assign new level numbers to each feature or change of deposit as it was encountered – without regard to levels being assigned in other parts of the site. Thus there was no necessary relationship between, for example, area A level 10 and area B level 10. Each depended on the history of past activity in that part of the site. In the Mediterranean the problem was made more acute because of the large number of finds made, whether of pottery or

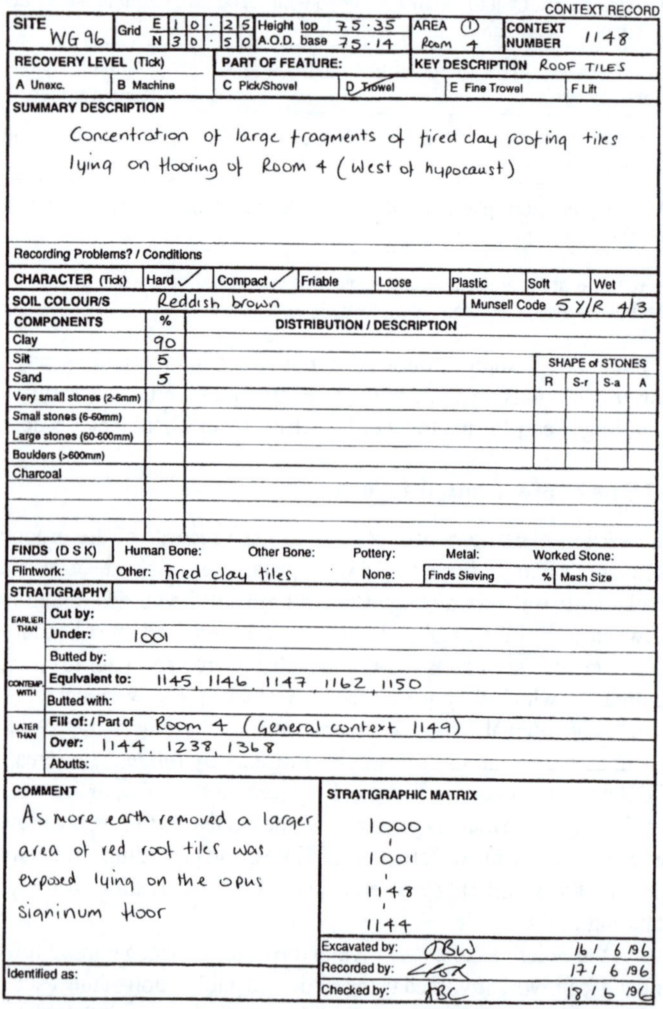

CONTEXT RECORD

SITE WG 96 | Grid E 1 0 · 2 5 N 3 0 · 5 0 | Height top 75·35 A.O.D. base 75·14 | AREA ① Room 4 | CONTEXT NUMBER 1148

RECOVERY LEVEL (Tick) | PART OF FEATURE: | KEY DESCRIPTION ROOF TILES

A Unexc. | B Machine | C Pick/Shovel | D Trowel | E Fine Trowel | F Lift

SUMMARY DESCRIPTION
Concentration of large fragments of fired clay roofing tiles lying on flooring of Room 4 (West of hypocaust)

Recording Problems? / Conditions

CHARACTER (Tick) | Hard ✓ | Compact ✓ | Friable | Loose | Plastic | Soft | Wet

SOIL COLOUR/S Reddish brown | Munsell Code 5Y/R 4/3

COMPONENTS	%	DISTRIBUTION / DESCRIPTION
Clay	90	
Silt	5	
Sand	5	
Very small stones (2-6mm)		
Small stones (6-60mm)		
Large stones (60-600mm)		
Boulders (>600mm)		
Charcoal		

SHAPE of STONES: R | S-r | S-a | A

FINDS (D S K) | Human Bone: | Other Bone: | Pottery: | Metal: | Worked Stone:
Flintwork: | Other: Fired clay tiles | None: | Finds Sieving | % | Mesh Size

STRATIGRAPHY
EARLIER THAN — Cut by: | Under: 1001 | Butted by:
CONTEMP. WITH — Equivalent to: 1145, 1146, 1147, 1162, 1150 | Butted with:
LATER THAN — Fill of: / Part of Room 4 (General context 1149) | Over: 1144, 1238, 1368 | Abutts:

COMMENT
As more earth removed a larger area of red roof tiles was exposed lying on the opus signinum floor

STRATIGRAPHIC MATRIX
1000
1001
1148
1144

Identified as:

Excavated by: JBW 16/6/96
Recorded by: LFGK 17/6/96
Checked by: ABC 18/6/96

Fig 6.2 The front of a context record sheet used at the Whitely Grange Roman Villa provides information about the location, nature and relationships of each deposit.

other materials. Here it became customary to record a **basket** number in addition to the **level** number, so that material from a single part of a larger level could be separately identified and tracked through the finds study process.

In response to these problems, the system of recording by **contexts** was developed. Each context is a logical unit of excavation – a new

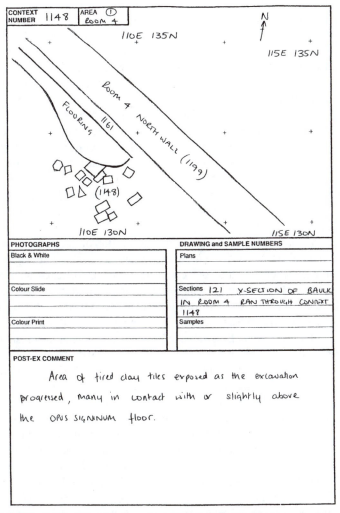

Fig 6.3 The back of the sheet provides for a sketch of the features discovered, together with a record of photographs and drawings. Post-ex(cavation) comment(s) reflect the retrospective assessment of the significance of each context.

deposit, the destruction debris on the floor of a room, a pit, ditch or a grave. Each context is given a unique number and all finds made in it as well as all records made of it are related to that number so that it is easy in retrospect during the study to discover what objects were associated with each other and the nature of the deposit in which they were found.

The method is relatively easy to apply in area excavation, where it is usually possible to identify and plan a complete context *before* its excavation, since the workforce can continue in another area while the record is being made. The record can then be enlarged as the context is being dug away, and thus better understood, and completed once it has been finally removed. For example, a strip of differently coloured earth across part of the site may be clearly visible so that its outline can be planned and a context number assigned. At this stage it will be called no more than a **feature**. Excavation will then remove part so that the nature of the soil within the feature can be described and the edges can be explored to discover whether they are vertical or irregular – revealing perhaps whether it is a narrow drainage channel or the 'bedding trench' for the horizontal timber ('sleeper beam') at the base of a wall in timber-framed buildings. Finally, once the feature has been emptied, the plan will be revised, the cross-section will be drawn and the context description completed and filed.

In Mediterranean conditions where excavation of deep sites is more common and area excavation thus restricted, it is often impossible to complete the identification of a complete context before excavation has to proceed. The recording method may therefore need to be adapted to take account of this factor as well as the quantity of finds. At Assiros for example, it was decided to base the recording system on the **baskets** used for pottery collection. Excavation of each deposit or feature was started with a unique numbered basket which was used until the feature had been completely excavated or until it was full, when a new basket was started with a new unique number. A separate record sheet (Fig. 6.4) was kept for each basket which indicated its location within the feature, as well as all the details about the character of the soil and the finds made. The area supervisor would then complete a summary description of each context (usually described as a 'level') with details of the baskets and **basket numbers** used to excavate it. All finds made in addition to the pottery were related to the basket number so that their closer and wider associations within the feature could be readily established.

Whichever system is employed the aim is the same: the full description of the soils excavated and the features encountered, whether they are constructions such as walls, cuts such as pits or ditches, or simply

man-made or natural deposits encountered in exploring the site. All artefacts, whether pottery, stone, bone or metal, all environmental material
collected, such as animal bones or charred seeds, and all samples for
study (Carbon 14 dating, phosphate analysis etc) must be entered on the
context or basket record sheets. The same is true for other kinds of record
such as photographs, plans or sections. Study and analysis of finds is

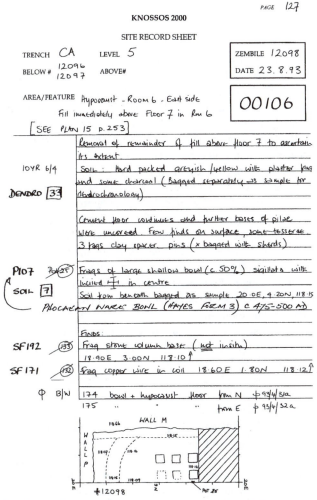

KNOSSOS 2000

PAGE 127

SITE RECORD SHEET

TRENCH CA   LEVEL 5

BELOW # 12096 12097   ABOVE#

ZEMBILE 12098

DATE 23.8.93

AREA/FEATURE Hypocaust - Room 6 - East side
Fill immediately above Floor 7 in Rm 6

00106

[SEE PLAN 15 p.253]

Removal of remainder of fill above floor 7 to ascertain
its extent

10YR 6/4   SOIL : Hard packed greyish/yellow with plaster frag
and some charcoal (Bagged separately as sample for

DENDRO 33   dendrochronology)

Cement floor continues and further bases of pilae
were uncovered. Few finds on surface, some tesserae.
3 frags clay spacer pins (x bagged with sherds)

P107   Pot 25   Frags of large shallow bowl (c 50%) sigillata with
incised ++ in centre

SOIL 7   Soil from beneath bagged as sample 20.0E, 4.20N, 118.15
PHOCAEAN WARE BOWL (HAYES FORM 3) c 475-500 AD

FINDS :

SF192   133   Frag stone column base (not in situ)
18.90E   3.00N   118.10↑

SF171   132   Frag copper wire in coil   18.60E   1.80N   118.12↑

φ   B/W   174   bowl + hypocaust   floor   from N   φ 93/4/31a
175   "   "   from E   φ 93/4/32a

Fig. 6.4 A *zembile* (basket) record sheet used on site at Knossos records the
location of the deposit, the nature and results of the work in progress and the finds
made. It is accompanied by a diagram of the trench showing the area under
excavation and the depth reached at its base.

quicker and more effective if all this information is systematically entered in the same place – even though the detail may well be repeated in other finds or environmental records.

The examples of completed recording sheets given (Figs. 6.2, 6.3 and 6.4) should be self explanatory; it is customary to have a more detailed sheet for recording features where a context is more complex than a level or spread of material.

6.3 Photography

The value of photography to the archaeologist was recognised almost from its invention, and by the late nineteenth century photographs formed a vital part of almost every archive and excavation report. At first the technique was used sparingly: even when photography had progressed from wet negative plates – which had to be prepared on site – to large-format glass plates, the cameras and the other equipment were relatively bulky and expensive. Since the invention of a celluloid film base and the development of sophisticated small format (35mm.) cameras, however, there has been no excuse for inadequate photography of site or finds. The rapid reduction in the cost of colour photography has also had an enormous impact, both in interpretation and in presentation of results. Today the development of the digital camera has added another dimension: everything can now be photographed readily and stored and indexed conveniently. At the same time the use of video records to allow the creation of moving panoramas or the effect of walking round the subject matter provides a perspective on the discoveries previously only available to those who took part.

There are many excellent books on technical aspects of photography and there is only enough space here to explain the procedures necessary for *archaeological* photography. First of all, a good camera is essential: its cost is minimal in relation to the cost of the project as a whole. Opinion is still divided about the relative quality of digital and conventional cameras and how well photographs taken in colour can be converted into the black-and-white images required for most publications. For the archaeologist, the advantages of cost and storage space, as well as the ability to manipulate the images, will probably result in the general adoption of the digital camera very soon. Whichever type of camera is chosen, it must have a single lens reflex system or digital equivalent. It is vital to be able to see exactly the image you are about to photograph. The camera chosen must have a good wide angle lens for work on site (especially in narrow trenches) and a good close-up lens for photographing small objects such as coins. Many projects will invest in two or three cameras, to make sure work is never held up.

The subject to be photographed, whether a mosaic floor within the aisle of a church or a group of shattered pottery vessels on a destruction floor, must be properly prepared – swept or scraped clean with a clear margin free from unwanted tools, equipment or unsightly tapes or strings. If these must be left in place, they must be neat and tidy. It is surprising how much that is not seen through the lens – a pair of shoes in the corner of the picture or a wheelbarrow on the edge of the trench – will appear in the developed image! Some directors insist on a swept or manicured free margin around the trench containing the subject of photography. Although it is now possible to 'improve' images digitally and to remove extraneous shoes or other unwanted items, this is regarded as sharp practice. The old belief that 'the photograph never lies' should still be taken as axiomatic in archaeological work.

Careful consideration must be given to the time of day when the photograph will be taken, especially in Mediterranean countries where sunshine is normal. Strong sun results in strong shadows which even digital techniques can only penetrate with difficulty (Fig. 6.5). Photographs are better taken on overcast days (one of the few advantages of British archaeological conditions), or early in the morning and late in the evening when the sun is not casting shadows at all. In such cases it will be essential to use a tripod with a conventional camera to enable a sufficiently long exposure in poor light without 'camera shake'. Flash equipment can be used to help 'fill in' small shadowed areas with some success but is not generally applicable. Organising work so that the site is clean at the optimum time for photography, especially on a windy day, can be very difficult. One of the greatest problems for archaeologists is that differences in the colour of newly exposed surfaces are quickly bleached out by strong sunshine.

Consideration must always be given to the purpose of the photograph in selecting the appropriate angle(s) and the amount to be included. Good photographs are immediately intelligible: bad ones may show nothing more than a broken pot in an empty space. Sometimes a series of photographs focussing in on a particular feature or features within a room or building will be helpful in understanding the situation. The video record is particularly good for 'zooming in' in this kind of situation.

When the optimum time has been chosen and the subject is clean, the area can be prepared for the actual photograph by adding 'ranging poles' (striped surveyors' poles) that act as scales. These should be placed on the ground parallel with the line of view and at right angles to it, to indicate

Fig 6.5 Photograph with strong contrast between light and shade obscuring the features it was intended to illustrate. The lack of a scale and reference information will make it hard to identify later and difficult to interpret.

Fig 6.6 Photograph with even lighting, scales, north point and reference number. Knossos, Roman buildings second century AD.

the dimensions of the feature being photographed. If there are standing walls, a vertical pole may also be helpful but the angle of this and the other poles must be adjusted so that they look right in the viewfinder. Finally, a north point and an identification code or number should be added; this may be chalked on a blackboard or formed with neatly painted numbers (Fig. 6.6). Hours can be wasted later if this simple provision is forgotten since identifying site photographs from memory is not always easy. If a second view point has been selected, the poles and numbers may have to be moved to reflect this. The identification number(s) should be recorded in an index and added to the relevant context sheets so that later cross-referencing is straightforward.

Ideally, the feature should not be disturbed until the photographic record has been checked: even better, not before a print has been added to the site record and annotated against the context sheets. In recent years an instant Polaroid photograph was the simplest way of achieving this, but digital images can be produced almost as quickly.

Object photography is both harder and less complicated. A clean background, a tripod, two or four adjustable lights and a methodical approach should result in adequate photographs; usually it does just that and achieves photographs suitable for the record. Good photographs with the proper balance of light and shadow to bring out the character of an object are much more difficult to attain. Here the professional photographer comes into his own. Should you take your own record photographs remember to include a simple scale and reference number with every object. Confusion is, regrettably, never far away, especially with large numbers of similar items.

6.4 Plans

No record can be complete without the inclusion of plans of individual features or the site as a whole. With a neat hand and a little arithmetic and geometry, together with a careful, methodical approach, planning is a skill most archaeologists and assistants can master.

The first essential is the concept of scale – the relationship between the size of the feature on the ground and on the graph paper of the plan. A common planning scale is 1:20 – that is to say 1cm. on the plan represents 20cm. on the ground or, put another way, 1m. on the ground appears as 5cm. on the plan. The scale can be marked out on the graph paper in advance, or transferred with the aid of a scale rule (a three-sided ruler with six different scales available – make sure you always use the same one!). One of the commonest errors in planning is to mistake the scale for one vital measurement and then spend hours wondering why the plan does not look right. An error often made by beginners is to attempt a level of accuracy which is impossible and unnecessary. Take your pencil for example: draw a line and work out what thickness it represents on the ground. At 1mm. thick, it reflects 2cm. at a scale of 1:20. Remember that most plans will be reduced for publication, to 50% or less of their drawn size.

A few simple principles of geometry are also very useful and, for the *Classical* archaeologist, expected. After all, it was Pythagoras who taught us that any triangle with sides of 3:4:5 had a right angle between the two shorter sides and Euclid who established that if the lengths of all three sides of a triangle are known, only two triangles can be drawn, the one the mirror image of the other. The first principle is basic to planning by offsets, the second to triangulation.

The first step is to set out a grid or base line across a site with the aid of a theodolite, level or EDM (see Chapter 4.3) to which the plans of individual features can be made. The simplest methods of site-planning involve the use of measuring-tapes which must be kept taut and horizontal in order to secure the most accurate measurements. In Britain, long steel tapes are not usually subject to the shrinking and stretching which can affect traditional cloth measuring-tapes. In the heat of the Mediterranean summer, however, they expand unacceptably and modern fibreglass tapes are more reliable.

The off-set method of feature drawing uses measuring-tapes to record short distances from a fixed baseline (Fig. 6.7). Such measurements must be taken at right-angles to the baseline: this can be ensured by using an optical square (a tiny prism which enables the user to look along a line and see what is at 90°), or by creating a triangle with sides in the proportions 3:4:5 with tapes and then marking the line of the perpendicular with a peg or ranging rod. Alternatively, a tape fixed at one end on the point to be measured can be swung back and forth over the baseline until the shortest measurement is obtained, automatically forming a right angle. In practice the experienced planner with 'his eye in' can judge the right angle with satisfactory accuracy.

In the triangulation method, two tapes running from fixed points along the baseline are crossed over the point to be planned and measurements taken (Fig. 6.8). Having three known sides of the triangle, the position of the point can easily be transferred to a plan using compasses and a rule. (Check that your triangle is on the right side of the base line.) In order for these planning methods to remain accurate all tapes must be kept level, so measurements taken on a slope will require the use of a spirit level

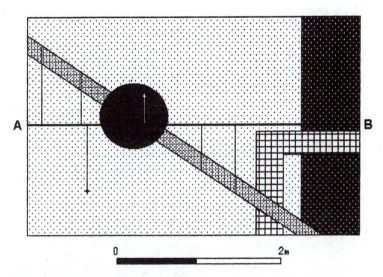

Fig 6.7 Planning using the offset method. A string (A-B) and tape have been set out across the trench and measurements have been taken at right angles to the string to record the positions of small finds and a drain.

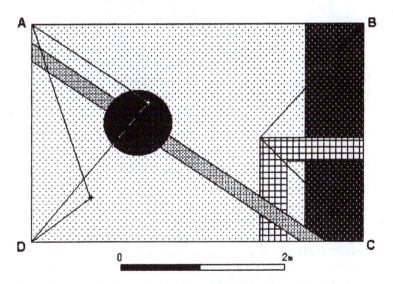

Fig 6.8 Planning using the triangulation method. Tapes are used to measure distances from known points (in this case the corners of the trench) to record positions of small finds and the corner of a wall. Two measurements are needed for each location.

and a plumb-bob (thin line with a conical weight on the end) to position the point to be read accurately along the baseline.

Where there is considerable detail to be recorded on a relatively level surface, such as a cobbled floor or yard surface scattered with debris, it will speed up the process if a planning frame is used (Fig. 6.9). This is usually a square wooden or metal frame measuring 1m. each way, with

Fig 6.9 The use of a planning frame: Whitely Grange Roman Villa, Wroxeter.

strings (ideally elastic) 10cm. or 20cm. apart across it in both directions. The corners are set against predetermined grid points and the detail of the surface is drawn in by eye against the grid squares of the graph paper.

The recording, drawing and photography of graves is a particularly important task, as the orientation of the burial and the presence or absence of grave goods may give vital information concerning the ritual associated with the burial – and consequent indications of date – since Christian burials are usually oriented east-west and devoid of grave goods. Photography (vertical and, if available, colour stereoscopic) of the skeleton *in situ* is crucial, as is careful drawing. Special skeleton recording sheets, where the surviving bones and associated finds can be added to a pre-printed diagram of a skeleton, can greatly speed up the process of recording (see Fig. 5.5). With cemeteries, each grave's orientation and relationship to other graves on the site must be accurately recorded so that, for example, groups of burials or changes in use over time may be studied. It is not unusual to find burials cut into and across earlier burials in cemeteries which were used over long periods of time.

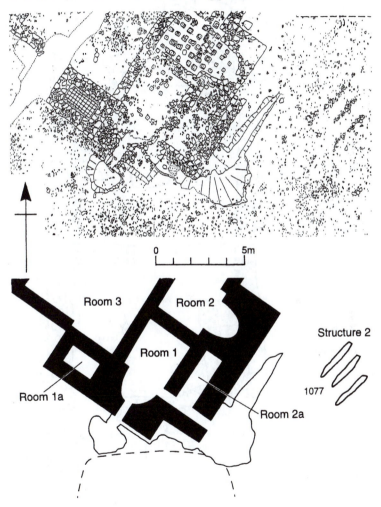

Fig 6.10 Part of the bath suite at Whitely Grange Roman Villa, as planned stone by stone using a planning frame (opposite) simplified to make the building plan comprehensive (overleaf). Interpretation of this kind is almost always necessary in planning since the preservation of different parts of the same building can be so variable.

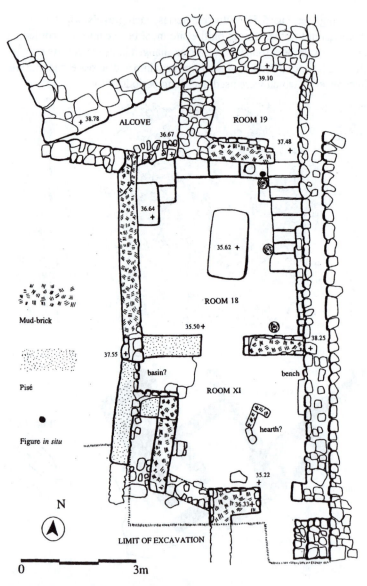

Fig 6.11 A detailed plan of the Temple at Mycenae showing the mud brick, *pise* (rammed clay) and stone used in different parts of the construction. Triangulation was used for this plan since the walls still stand up to 2m. in height. Spot heights obtained with the aid of a level or water level show the different floor levels and the height to which the walls are preserved in different places. Thicker lines are used to distinguished the edges of walls as appropriate.

Photogrammetry (measurement from rectified photographic images) can also be employed to create plans where there is a considerable amount of detail to be scaled down, such as the mosaic floors at Çiftlik. This uses the techniques already described for aerial photography (Chapter 4.2), but obviously at a much closer range. As with every photographic technique it is important that wherever possible the results should be available before the features have been removed by further excavation.

Once the positions of the features on the horizontal plan have been recorded, the detail must be completed with conventions (shading or stippling) of different types to distinguish the different deposits and a key provided to explain them. It is usual to emphasise the edges of walls and other strong features to make sure they stand out more clearly. It is equally important to provide spot-heights or levels on the surfaces and features to show the extent of any slope and the height to which walls are standing or pits have been cut. Visualising the buildings recorded on any plan is much easier if the different levels are clearly differentiated. (See examples in Figs. 6.10 and 6.11.)

These levels may be obtained with the aid of a surveyor's level (as described in Chapter 4.3) or, much less accurately, with a 'bubble' level attached to a string led from a datum point. A simple method of obtaining readings accurate to within a centimetre which can be used over short distances – such as the depths of levels excavated or objects located within a single trench or excavation area – is provided by a water level (Fig. 6.12). This is a clear polythene tube 6-8m. in length, fastened to a wooden pole with a measuring-tape attached and filled with coloured water. Provided care is taken to avoid bubbles, the absolute level of the water at either end of the tube is identical, and a simple comparison can be made between the 'local' datum point (perhaps a nail in the trench side) and the object or feature to be levelled. Unfamiliar in Britain, this is a technique regularly used by Mediterranean builders, who may well be employed as workmen on site: for once, only the archaeologist needs to learn its application.

Site plans and **sections** (below) must always be checked on site, even if they are worked up in the drawing office before this. Queries all too often arise later – especially when two adjacent plans have to be joined – and a final check while the features still exist, or before they are covered over again, may prevent problems later. Each plan must be identified: with the site and area name, with the context numbers of deposits and features shown, with the scale and a north point, and finally with the name of the author and date of completion.

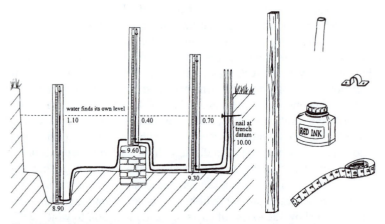

Fig 6.12 A water level is a practical substitute for expensive equipment. The height determined is the trench datum minus the reading on the tape measure. (In this diagram the trench datum is 10 m. above site datum, see Chapter 4.3.) To make one all you need is a 2m. length of wood 2-3cm. square, a 1.5m. dressmaker's tape measure, 6-8m. of clear plastic tubing, electrical cable clips and drawing pins. The tube is filled with water, coloured with red ink.

Fig 6.13 Earthquake traces in section at Ciftlik. The wall on the right has tilted over the fallen roof tiles and was later covered by successive layers of land slip and hill wash.

6.5 Sections

An archaeological section is the vertical record of the stratigraphy, the history of a site from its establishment to the modern surface (Fig. 6.13). This can be seen in the sides of the trenches or can sometimes be provided 'accidentally' before excavation starts, e.g. if the site has been cut by the engineering works for a road, eroded by the sea, or penetrated by a deep pit, such as a Victorian cellar. In such cases close study will repay the effort many times over, since the section provides a preview of what is still buried. As with plans, care and method are vital. It is essential that the drawing is an accurate record of changes in soil colour and texture, of fragments of masonry or rubble, of pits or cuttings, and walls or floor surfaces, but often a degree of interpretation (see Chapter 7.1) is necessary before the section drawing can be completed. Not all the boundaries between one deposit and another are clear and detective work is often necessary to establish where they were – on the basis of clues such as lines of ash or pebbles. A section drawing, even more than a plan, must make clear what is definite and what is tentative. The aim of the draughtsman should be to enable the section to be reassessed later without prejudice, in case the story it tells has been misunderstood. A few simple principles make the task easier:

- Work from the obvious towards the uncertain so that the problem area is defined as closely as possible.

- Follow the boundaries of deposits all the way round the trench or excavated area – you should return to the point at which you started. If you do not you have made a mistake.

- Look out for levels that stop suddenly: they may have been cut by a pit or ditch which is not immediately obvious. If several levels stop at the same point there must have been such an archaeological feature unless the phenomenon can be explained by natural action (earthquake or landslide).

- Remember that cuttings may indicate the removal of a wall or structure and explain a floor that goes nowhere.

The method of recording is relatively simple. A horizontal datum line is set at a convenient height across the section to be drawn and a long measuring-tape is fixed just above or below it to provide a horizontal scale. The measure is most readily fixed to long nails driven into the section with clothes pegs or bulldog clips. Offsets are measured up or down as appropriate with a short tape (a second datum line can be added if the section is very deep). A plumb-bob can be used to check the horizontal position of any feature against the measuring-tape. Given the detail to be recorded in many sections, a scale of 1:10 is often chosen. Wherever possible, coloured pencils are used to convey an impression of the soil colour, but conventions such as hatching can also be used.

6.6 First aid for finds (conservation)

Objects buried in the ground for centuries have often reached a state of chemical equilibrium. Decay and corrosion may have been rapid initially, but a stable state is eventually reached which is frequently maintained until the archaeologist intervenes and brings the objects to the light of day. Some objects which have had no exposure to the air since burial will start to change, especially if they have been waterlogged and start to dry out, or if they have been desiccated and are suddenly exposed to humidity. All need immediate remedial treatment if they are not to disintegrate and/or alter beyond recognition. In ideal circumstances a trained conservator will be part of the team – or at least on call no more than an hour or two away. Circumstances are, however, rarely ideal and the archaeologist will often be faced with the need to take preventative action so that the objects in question can reach the stabilising conditions of a conservation laboratory as safely as possible. Preventative action should always be based on a minimalist and reversible approach rather than the 'amateur' application of chemicals or treatments. A conservator should always be consulted in advance about recommended first aid treatments since new materials and processes are being developed all the time. Part of the planning process should involve research into likely finds and their condition, together with the kind of storage available and the proximity of expert help.

Pottery is usually no problem on Classical sites since it is hard-fired, inert and almost indestructible, although some soil conditions can reduce even the best quality to a soft soapy condition. It can normally be washed without difficulty provided caution is used where the paint has been added after firing or there is a paste fill. Stone objects are often in good condition but can be very friable if they have been exposed to heat (disastrous for sandstone and marble) or acidic conditions (which cause limestone and marble to disintegrate). Metals like bronze or iron may well start to oxidise once exposed to air. Glass can be very fragile or surprisingly tough – depending on its composition and the burial conditions.

Bone or ivory will dry out after excavation and split into small fragments. Bone preserved in a damp environment (such as the skeletons found on the ancient waterfront at Herculaneum, for example) will need to be kept damp for some time to prevent rapid drying which is likely to cause cracking. This is particularly true in the case of burials where the bones are often fragile and may need to be stabilised in the ground (often by painting on acrylic resin which is then allowed to dry and harden), or may be lifted within a block of soil. Further consolidation is likely to be needed and ideally the conservator is summoned to take care of this treatment, which must as far as possible avoid prejudicing future scientific analysis.

Items from waterlogged conditions such as leather or wood need specialist treatment from the outset. Excavation of waterlogged sites should not be attempted without the constant presence of a conservator. Among the greatest problems are those presented by such discoveries as wall-paintings *in situ*. Normally these must be removed by an expert and transferred to a specialist workroom, but the process is painstaking and laborious.

On site the first priority is the record of the object *in situ*: this may sometimes be all that will survive. In this situation there can hardly be too many photographs, plans and sketches: even when the object can be conserved, the conservator will want to know all the circumstances of its burial and uncovering. Speed is vital – delicate objects should never be left to dry out, especially not in the full sun. If necessary re-bury them until conditions are right later in the day. A plastic sheet for a cover will only cause the objects to sweat and encourage mould growth.

Once recorded, fragile objects should be lifted with the matrix of earth which supports them so that excavation can take place in the laboratory under controlled conditions. If absolutely necessary, the earth matrix (rather than the delicate object itself) can be consolidated with resin or supported with plaster. More robust materials, such as metals, can usually be detached from the matrix and wrapped in acid-free tissue as the first stage of preparation for transport. They should then be stored in slightly humid conditions and prevented from drying out. Objects of bone, ivory or glass may well need more support and packing, but this too can only be of inert materials.

Whatever treatment is given to an object, by the field team or by an expert conservator, it is vital to record all the details of chemicals or techniques used or the fact that no treatment was given at all. Future conservation relies on a full 'case history'.

Even the expert is not always certain how to treat particular objects and may have to make a choice where two different materials are involved. A good example of this is the burial urn from a tenth-century

BC grave at Lefkandi on the island of Euboea in Greece. The cremated remains of a local chieftain had been wrapped in a shaggy garment and placed in a large bronze amphora. The copper salts from the amphora must have helped the unusual preservation of the textile in the damp conditions of burial, but textiles and bronze require very different treatment in the laboratory. To preserve both, as in this case, is a notable achievement.

One task that is often neglected or carried out in haste is **packing.** Whether an object has to be transported to a museum where study can continue or is to be put away for long-term storage, the appropriate packing materials are essential. Acid-free tissue, conservation quality plastic bags and labels, polystyrene packing or bubble wrap and a multitude of storage boxes of different sizes are all minor expenses in comparison to the cost of the project as a whole and the potential scientific value of the finds made.

6.7 Finds and the finds record

Every Classical city, town or farmstead produces a wealth of material and objects of different kinds. Each kind of object can illuminate a different part of the story of a site and the people who once lived and worked there. Every cemetery is likely, in the same way, to illuminate the fashions of life as well as the rituals of death, with the additional benefit for the archaeologist that complete objects will be found. In contrast, a settlement, of whatever size, will only reveal the refuse that was thrown away, shattered or broken, unless it suffered a disaster which left the furniture in place and the provisions still in the storerooms, as at Pompeii and Akrotiri. The durable materials found in 'normal' excavation conditions include clay and stone, metal and glass, bone and ivory.

It is no small part of the work of the excavator to ensure that material of this kind, whether broken or complete, is systematically recorded on site and in the workroom so that its full significance can be evaluated. Each kind of object may be treated differently, depending on its frequency and condition as already described, but all must be fully labelled so that their identity and origin is permanently recorded.

Each find considered important enough to be treated individually will be given an unique identification number in addition to its context number. Good labelling with durable plastic labels or plastic bags (silverfish are particularly partial to the ink on paper or cardboard labels) and waterproof, fadeproof ink will go a long way to prevent objects becoming unidentifiable and joining the host of 'stateless' items which frequent even the best-run museums, and might as well never have been dug up in the first place.

Pottery is usually the most abundant material on any excavation, ranging from large storage jars for oil, grain or wine to the delicate drinking cups which imitate metal vessels in use in wealthier houses. Plain domestic wares or specialised cooking wares are usually the most common types, while fine table wares are rarer. In some periods specialised perfume or oil bottles were regularly used. Sometimes whole vessels will be found or groups of sherds which indicate a vessel shattered where it had stood. These will always merit individual treatment, from detailed drawings and photographs to separate registration numbers – and ultimately, if special, a place in a museum display. On site their exact location is recorded together with the depth at which they were found and their association with, for example, a floor or other feature. Pottery sherds, however, found in their thousands on Classical sites rarely merit individual treatment. These, as already mentioned, are collected in batches according to context or basket and studied as groups.

Initial studies of the pottery, whether whole or broken, will divide it into ware categories (types of fabric) and into shapes according to likely function. The wares will reveal something about the place of manufacture (and there are several analytical techniques which can help to demonstrate this) and the patterns of trade which supplied the community, whether from local or distant workshops. The wares and shapes together will indicate the kinds of activity taking place in the vicinity, whether purely domestic or partly industrial. The quality of the pottery – highly decorated or purely utilitarian – may give some indication of the status and wealth of those who used it.

The pottery record made in the workroom will vary according to the period and region in question but the procedures are similar everywhere. For each batch a record will be made of the number of pieces of the different shapes made in each ware, so that a quantitative picture can be built up for comparison with other sites. The wares may be grouped by criteria such as place of manufacture (local or imported) or date. Batches of pottery more often than not include sherds of earlier periods (if these are present at the site) which have no more significance in the context in which they were found than the pebbles and stones associated with them. In many areas the dating of the different levels and buildings relies on the pottery found in them (see Chapter 7.4) and it is axiomatic that the latest item present dates the context as a whole. For this reason understanding of the features excavated may well depend on the prompt preliminary study of the pottery. An unexpected pottery date might well cause a re-evaluation of the date of particular features or buildings, and perhaps the recognition of previously unidentified stratigraphic problems.

One necessary task before the final pottery record is compiled is to spread out each batch with its neighbours from adjacent contexts, or from contexts above or below, in the attempt to find as many joins between fragments as possible. In this way a better understanding of whole shapes can be often be gained, although it will never be possible to find joins for the majority of sherds in this way. Whole vessels, whether found *in situ* or restored from scattered fragments, are usually a much better guide to the date of the contexts in which they were found than the single sherds, however numerous.

Clay lamps are well known as distinctive forms from the Archaic period on and become particularly important from the Hellenistic period, because like pottery they change in style frequently, and are often made in specialised workshops and widely traded. In the Byzantine period as olive oil-producing regions were lost to Arab conquest, lamps were increasingly replaced by candles. Lamps can therefore often provide a great deal of information about date and trade connections.

After pottery, clay roof-tiles are perhaps the most common items found from the Archaic period onwards. Although bulky, they will often repay study because they can indicate the style of roofing, the place of manufacture and, even, when stamped with a maker's mark, the rough date of manufacture. When buildings were replaced the roof-tiles, as at Çiftlik, were often re-used as hard-core for floor foundations, thus giving important insights about the overall chronology of sites. By the Roman period, especially in military and imperial contexts, the practice emerged of stamping bricks with marks indicating the maker or client, the date and batch. These, too, are extremely useful to archaeologists for indicating the date of buildings. They may also provide information, for instance, about the movement of the Roman legions whose stamps appear on the tiles. It is likely that only pieces with distinctive characteristics or stamps will be recorded separately, while often the remainder, once photographed or recorded on a plan, will be stacked on site – available for study but largely unloved.

Other items of clay which are frequently found include figurines of different kinds – often referred to as terracottas – loom weights, spindle whorls, fishing net weights, gaming pieces. Even clay bathtubs can be found on occasion. Each of these will be recorded with an exact position on site and usually given a separate register number. A group of loom weights, for example, may indicate where a loom had been in use.

There can be a wide range of stone objects, whole or broken off larger items. Many are only loosely identifiable as whetstones, sockets, grinding stones and the like; but some, such as pieces of architecture or sculpture, are immediately recognisable even if fragmentary. Diagnostic architectural fragments such as those from column capitals or architraves may well indicate the kind of structures which once stood in the vicinity and perhaps even their date. Roman-style millstones are unmistakable, while occasionally fragments of stone furniture are found. Another kind of stone object known from several Roman cities is the official standard of fluid measure used for both grain and liquids. Inscriptions may be found on tombstones or sarcophagi, but often on blocks re-used in later walling so that their original provenance is unknown. Some inscriptions will give the names and titles of the dead, some will list civic honours or privileges, while others may be graffiti or instructions to builders. At Knossos blocks of Roman date have been found with Greek annotations such as *pemptos apo dexia* – fifth from the right – one of the earliest examples of kit building. All such items will be separately recorded and registered in the excavation catalogue.

Seal- and ring-stones were carved in many periods and show the skills of the craftsmen who made these miniature works of art. Although they will always be registered separately, their 'life span' is so long that they will rarely be useful for chronological purposes. Beads of a wide variety of exotic stones such as lapis lazuli, carnelian, rock crystal or amethyst, as well as the fossilised resin, amber, are also quite common.

Metals are usually better represented in burial contexts than in settlements because, unless the graves have been robbed, there has been no attempt to recycle the metal. From the Classical period onwards the most common items recovered are iron nails and coins. The nails may come from sandals, furniture and coffins or from timber building elements, and their position may be significant although the individual items are unimpressive.

For many years, gold, silver or bronze coins with their inscriptions or readily identifiable symbols were preferred to pottery as dating evidence, even though a single coin can remain in circulation a long time or can find its way *down* through the stratigraphy as a result of root action or burrowing animals. Even so, their potential for illuminating political relationships in the Classical and Hellenistic periods or economic conditions in the Roman imperial period is unrivalled. For these reasons, the find-spots of coins are always recorded in detail, and they are registered individually. Once cleaned, it may be appropriate to make plaster casts or foil impressions of coins to enable further study, while coin photography is a highly skilled technique.

The range of other metal items is almost endless, whether gold or silver used for jewellery, or lead used for clamps and piping. Bronze and iron which was ubiquitous since the tenth century BC were used for an astonishing range of items: weapons and armour, craftsman's or agricultural tools, locks and keys for the front door or the treasure chest, jugs and drinking vessels, jewellery, lamps and lampstands, penholders and inkstands, writing styluses, fishhooks and darning needles, medical or musical instruments, statues, furniture and so on. All deserve detailed study and, at least in the later periods, most show the universality of fashion and technology within the Roman empire. Unfortunately in settlements, most of these are only represented by fragments and a great deal of expertise is necessary to identify the majority. Many scraps remain unidentifiable and are unlikely to be registered unless they originate from a hoard of material hidden away by a metalsmith for future use.

Bone and ivory were also widely used for small items such as decorative pins for the hair or the clothing, combs, spoons, ointment spatulae and gaming pieces. Other regular uses were for handles for knives or mirrors, or for the manufacture of pipes and other musical instruments. Ivory when acquired as large segments from the tusk could be used for the manufacture of cylindrical boxes, carved into figures of different kinds or even sections of furniture such as throne legs. The tomb of Philip II contained a magnificent couch with ivory carvings and fittings, and a shield embellished with figures in high relief. Both materials were employed as inlays for wooden boxes or furniture, or used in composite jewellery. Shell could sometimes be used in the same way but mostly turns up in excavations as food debris.

Glass evolved from an unusual material in the Bronze Age to a commonplace one in the Roman period. In sites of early periods every fragment will be significant, while often on a Roman site glass will deserve no more specialised treatment than pottery – except that it cannot be thrown into large baskets. Glass vessels were obviously in common use throughout the empire, though certain centres such as northern Italy and Syria were particularly noted for their specialised production of coloured glass of high quality. The Portland vase in the British Museum illustrates one end of the range. This is a large bowl made with two layers of glass of contrasting colours with the outer layer cut back to form a design in relief. The other is shown by *unguentaria*, often known as tear bottles. These long test-tube-like vessels found in many Roman graves, are both crudely blown and roughly finished. In public buildings of the Roman and early Byzantine periods glass lamp-bowls suspended in bronze chandeliers (*polycandela*) were normal, and these form the most common small objects found in early churches whose floors were swept clean of the debris which characterises domestic surfaces.

The presence of *tesserae*, cubes or chips of stone, clay or glass on some Hellenistic and many Roman sites many give early warning of mosaic pavements in the vicinity. Glass tesserae are usually from wall or ceiling mosaics and provide the luminous colours to be found in mosaics in late Roman and Byzantine churches such as at Ravenna, Thessaloniki and Constantinople. Individual pieces may be sorted by material and colour but individually are of little significance.

As already described, each type of object is capable of making a different contribution to understanding a site and the culture to which it belongs. Before this contribution can be evaluated, an objective record of each item must be made, in the same way as for the contexts and features on site (Fig. 6.14). Naturally the kind of information needed for each is different but some basic essentials are needed, including the details of the find-spot and context. For a metal object, for example, this information will include the kind of metal (bronze, iron, silver etc); the basic category (nail, buckle, lock plate); dimensions (length, width, diameter); manufacturing technique (hammered or cast); condition (intact, broken, corroded). Most objects will require a detailed description of shape and decoration, which may be supplemented by sketches or scale drawings (Fig. 6.16) and photographs of different views as appropriate.

This record may be made on prepared forms or cards, and is usually then entered into a computer database to enable rapid retrieval and sorting. Provision should be made for additional categories of information such as conservation treatment, scientific analysis, and the location of publication photographs and drawings as well as the location of the object itself on the storeroom shelf or in a museum exhibition. It is important that a *paper* record should be made of all these details as well as a digital one, for convenience as much as to avoid computer failure, since there may well be periods on remote excavation sites where the electricity supply or an individual piece of equipment fails.

Whether each category of material is recorded on a form of a different style, or whether a single type of record sheet is used for all registered finds, it is important that the site context sheets are annotated with the final brief description of the item and that a consolidated index is kept (Fig. 6.15). In situations where a local representative is responsible for the safe-keeping of the finds made until they are handed over to the local museum at the end of the season, a single master register is essential to avoid any misunderstandings.

SPECIAL FINDS RECORD

SITE W697	AREA WEST	FROM CONTEXT 1001 / 1304	SPECIAL FIND NUMBER 696

CO-ORDINATES E 96·64	N 89·61	H 77·374	

MATERIAL BRONZE	TYPE COIN

COMPLETENESS reasonably complete

DESCRIPTION

" GALERIUS MAXIMIANUS "

Remnants of silver wash still visible

SKETCH OVER Y/N

LENGTH /	WIDTH /	THICKNESS 2	DIAM. 1·8

CONDITION In excellent condition – requires attention

TREATMENT ON SITE to reveal full details
Wrapped in acid-free tissue packed with
silica gel in plastic container

RECORDED BY Martin W#	DATE 26·6·97	BOX No.

CONSERVATION	DATE SENT:	DATE RETURNED:
LABORATORY	X-RAY PLATE No.	DATE

TREATMENT / ANALYSIS TYPE	DATE	LABORATORY	LAB. REF. No.	REPORT No.
1				
2				
3				

LENGTH /	WIDTH /	THICKNESS ·2	DIAM. 1·8	WEIGHT

SPECIALIST	DATE SENT:	DATE RETURNED:

CATALOGUE DESCRIPTION & IDENTIFICATION

PARALLELS

DATE RANGE	CATALOGUED BY:	DATE:
PHOTO	DRAWING Nos.: ARCHIVE	PUBLICATION

Version –June1991

Birmingham University Field Archaeology Unit

Fig 6.14 Finds recording sheet – Whitely Grange Roman Villa, Wroxeter. The initial record of the find spot, description and treatment of this Roman coin was made on site and will be supplemented during conservation and final study.

6.8 The environmental record

The application of environmental studies to sites of the Classical or later periods in the Mediterranean area is a relatively recent phenomenon, whereas in Britain they have been employed for much longer. There is in contrast, for the prehistoric period from the beginning of the Neolithic onwards, abundant evidence about the crops grown and the animals exploited in Greece and Turkey.

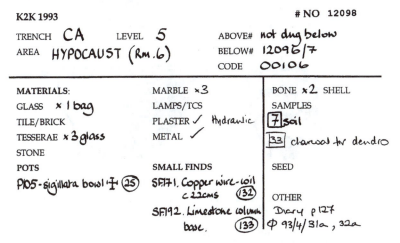

Fig 6.15 Summary finds record for each context – Knossos. Each category of object listed here from pots to samples is separately studied and recorded in detail elsewhere.

It is an accepted principle that man's exploitation of the environment is intimately related to the nature of that environment. Any archaeological project needs to consider the conditions which may have existed during occupation or use of the site or region together with any changes which may have taken place during the period of occupation or use. Naturally, the evidence is, as in so many areas of study of the past, far less than explicit. At the same time the evidence of the nature of the exploitation should be actively sought and this is best done by seeking the collaboration of one or more specialists in this field: geographers, palaeozoologists, and palaeobotanists.

Study of the present-day landscape can often provide clues about its past character in terms of patterns of erosion and deposition which may be detectable. The level of forestation at any period is harder to establish, though ancient pollen from lake-bed cores, and charcoal fragments from fuel or building timbers from the excavation can tell us about the kinds

Pottery vessels are drawn as if one quarter was cut away to show the thickness of the vessel wall and the decoration on both the exterior *and* the interior. True three dimensional drawings, (below left), in contrast, require much more skill but can obscure the detail and are harder to 'read'.

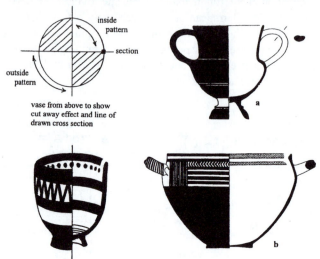

inside pattern

section

outside pattern

vase from above to show cut away effect and line of drawn cross section

a

b

Standard conventions mean that an archaeologist can 'read' the drawing below without the added annotations. Cross sections show the thickness of the different parts and additional views explain the details.

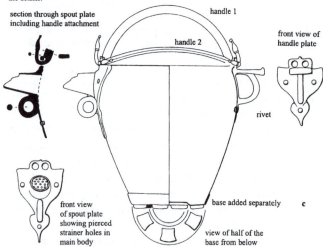

section through spout plate including handle attachment

handle 1

handle 2

front view of handle plate

rivet

front view of spout plate showing pierced strainer holes in main body

base added separately

c

view of half of the base from below

Fig 6.16 Drawing conventions: a) Corinthian Geometric *skyphos* (rim d. 17 cm.); b) Late Classical *kantharos* (rim d. 7 cm.); c) Late Classical *kadiskos*: bronze vessel with strainer spout and a pair of bucket handles (ht. 15.5 cm.). All from Vitsa cemetery, Epirus.

of trees present. The range of hunted animals in the faunal record from the site will also give some indication of the kind of habitat in the vicinity of the site, whether dense or open woodland. Finally, dendro-chronological samples (Chapter 7.4) may indicate how different the climate was and how prone to fluctuation.

Animal bone recovery is now normal on most excavations. Animal bones are collected separately from other materials, since they are relatively fragile, and some indication of quantity may be put on the context sheet. Like everything else, it is the context number which later identifies the group of bones during study. The extent to which sieving with a standard mesh sieve is used to obtain a systematic sample of the material present is variable.

With a good-sized sample (thousands rather than hundreds of identifiable fragments) it becomes possible to calculate significant ratios of the different types of animals domesticated (cattle, pigs, sheep and goats) and, with luck, to discover the age/sex ratios which may indicate the purpose for which the animals were kept. For example, the killing age of animals kept for meat only is relatively young and often has no specific sex bias. A high proportion of elderly sheep could indicate flocks kept for wool. Middle-aged female cattle are likely to have been milk producers, while older male specimens were probably kept alive to serve as beasts of burden or for ploughing. The wild animals present indicate the level of hunting as a supplement to the diet (deer, wild boar, hare) or that they were valued for their skins (lynx, bear, fox). Beaver, otter and the bones of such birds as geese and herons may well indicate wetlands nearby.

The recovery of plant remains is more complex. Special conditions are necessary for organic materials of this type to survive at all. Most commonly, grain, seeds and other vegetable matter are preserved as charcoal as a consequence of accidental charring during food preparation or by a major destruction which affected crops in storage (Fig. 6.17). More rarely, seeds can be incorporated in mud-brick or other building materials, or in pottery during manufacture so that their impressions survive.

Although charred grain can often be seen in different deposits and levels, conventional dry sieving would soon destroy the fragile seeds. To overcome this problem, special flotation sieves have been developed which use a strong jet of air bubbled through a tank of water. A sample (2-4 bucketsful) of earth is poured gradually into the top of the tank and the bubbles help break up the soil and release the light charcoal particles which are then collected in a fine-meshed sieve. When dried, not only can the seeds of cereals and other plants be carefully separated from the debris, but so can fragments of the ears of wheat or barley (the chaff) which are often more informative about the precise species than the grain itself.

Typical crops which have been identified in this way in the Mycenaean period include cereals such as wheat, barley and millet, legumes such as lentils, peas, chickpeas and vetch, 'tree' crops such as grapes, olives and figs, together with a wide range of wild resources which were exploited. Once a site has been sampled systematically, the technique of

Fig 6.17 Fragments of ears of wheat, only partly threshed for better resistance to insects and moulds. Assiros c. 1300 BC.

presence analysis (the calculation of the proportion of samples from each period which contain a specific crop type) allows the popularity of different crop types to be determined and information from different sites to be compared.

Soil samples can also be processed to retrieve **pollen** samples. Pollen is microscopic, but remarkably durable. Its study is the province of specialists (palynologists) whose analysis can yield conclusions about levels of agricultural activity and relative densities of different plant species. In situations where there is knowledge about the date of introduction of particular species to different areas, as with the Roman introduction of crop and garden plants to Britain, study of pollen can provide an indication about the dating of a site from which no artefacts have been retrieved.

If circumstances do not allow the inclusion of an environmental recovery team as part of the project, a minimum level of sample can be achieved simply by bagging large samples of earth from each likely looking context for later laboratory examination. Whichever method is used, it is important to keep an accurate record – not only of the context from which the sample(s) were taken but also of the precise location, using a special recording sheet if appropriate.

Chapter 7
Study, analysis and presentation

Although an archaeological excavation is the culmination of a long period of preparation, excavation and recording are far from the end of a research project. The ultimate goal is publication – at a variety of levels. The most detailed reports are for other archaeologists who will wish to study the results for themselves. Outline publications are essential to interest and inform a general public whose taxes ultimately support most research. It may also be necessary to cater for the needs of different interest groups, ranging from professional ceramic specialists to residents who wish to know more about the archaeology of the area where they live.

Information recorded about the site and the finds must be digested before final conclusions can be drawn. A period of study and analysis inevitably intervenes between excavation and publication. The architecture of any buildings and the sequence of levels (the **stratigraphy**) need to be reviewed. The finds made – whether pottery, metal, stone or other materials – need to be classified layer by layer and period by period. The resultant **typologies** (sequences of artefacts of different types) must be set out clearly so that they can be compared with those on other sites. With luck these typologies provide the basis for **dating** each layer – in relation to other sites or collections of finds and, sometimes, absolutely.

All this evidence, whether natural or man-made, will help to place the finds from each period in their historical context and thus enable the production of a coherent account of the results. One of the final stages of this analysis is **interpretation**: the attempt to understand what each complex of finds from a site tells us about the people who lived there and the different activities they pursued.

7.1 Stratigraphy

One of the harshest criticisms made of any field archaeologist is that he or she 'paid no attention to stratigraphy'. All too often this was true of excavations taking place in the eastern Mediterranean before the 1960s. It is no credit to Classical archaeology that techniques widely employed in Britain and Western Europe in the 1920s and 30s took so long to be put into practice. As already noted (Chapter 2.3) 'stratigraphic excavation' is essential in modern archaeology. The horizontal layers must be recorded as they are exposed, while the **sections**, the drawn record of the vertical sides of each trench or area of excavation, are vital evidence for interpreting the history of a site.

The science of 'stratigraphy' was developed simultaneously by archaeologists and geologists in the eighteenth and nineteenth centuries as they attempted to understand how the landscape was created and to estimate the time-scale for the major stages. Study of rock formations and river valleys or archaeological mounds revealed levels of deposition – laid down, geologically, by alluvial and seismic processes and, archaeologically, by successive phases of human occupation. This work gradually undermined the orthodox view that the world was created in seven days in 4004 BC, and the conclusion won wide acceptance following the revelation by Darwin and others of the evolution of different species over almost unimaginable periods of time.

The first methodical archaeologists, such as Pitt-Rivers in the 1860s, rapidly understood that the same principles could be as well applied to the formation of a single site as to the formation of the landscape as a whole. The only difference, apart from the time-scale involved, was that geological processes were natural while those that took place on a site were partly **anthropogenic** (resulting from human action) and partly natural. Sites vary considerably in depth depending on the building materials employed and the duration of occupation, but all are created by the same processes of human construction, use and destruction and by the same natural processes of decay, deposition and erosion. With these processes in mind it is possible to 'read' the stratigraphy of a section on site (or its reproduction on paper) and separate the different phases of its history – whether these resulted in the accumulation of fresh deposits or the cutting away of old ones.

The process is best understood by looking at an actual section-drawing. Figure 7.1 shows a section which was cut by the sea as it eroded the coastline at Çiftlik on the north side of the site. Artefacts which were retrieved from different contexts in the section demonstrate the obvious conclusion that the oldest levels are those at the bottom and the most recent levels are those at the top. 'Reading' the section enables us to appreciate the length of occupation at this site and changing patterns of human activity. Study of this section reveals how the its later phases exactly match those found by excavating the church to the south, but this section also proves that the site was occupied long before the church was constructed in the fourth century AD.

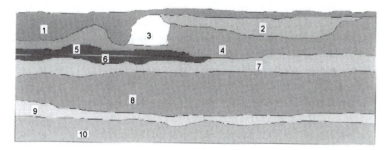

Fig 7.1 Interpreting a section – the cliff face at Ciftlik.

	Description	*Interpretation*
1	Modern topsoil (contains a variety of artefacts, both modern and ancient).	Ploughsoil with materials from various parts of the site.
2	Layer with pottery wasters and kiln material (fifth-sixth centuries AD).	Evidence of industrial activity.
3	Deposit of crumbled lime mortar.	Cut caused by robbing out a wall to retrieve stones for re-use and dumping the mortar back into the 'robber trench'.
4	Layer with pottery from fourth and fifth centuries AD.	Domestic occupation associated with building represented by robbed-out wall (3).
5	Layer of charcoal and ash.	Destruction deposit.
6	Layer of charcoal and ash.	Destruction deposit artificially levelled.
7	Layer with Roman local and imported pottery.	Occupation deposit.
8	Layer with pottery from fourth to second centuries BC.	Occupation deposit.
9	Layer with pottery from sixth and fifth centuries BC.	Occupation deposit.
10	Layer with Bronze Age pottery.	Occupation deposit.

NB Bottom of drawing represents sea level. It was impossible to reveal the bottom of level 10, or whether there was earlier occupation at the site.

Another criticism often made of field archaeologists by outsiders is that they are little more than building-site labourers. In truth (leaving aside the undeserved insult to members of the building trade), the field archaeologist would be better equipped if this was the case. Experience of the processes of construction is a great asset in untangling the history of buildings on any site. Since interpretation of sections is impossible without some understanding of these processes, the main stages in the history of a building are set out below. How many can be detected depends on the building materials used and the later history of the site:

Construction

- Site preparation: levelling, cutting back, building terraces.
- Foundations: trenches filled with rubble or masonry, or slots to receive timber beams (sleeper beams) and post pits to support timber uprights.
- Walls: stones, fired brick, sun-dried mud-brick with or without timber framing, 'wattle and daub', planking. Stone walls may or may not be bonded with clay or mortar.
- Roofs: pitched or flat; branches daubed with clay, timber and thatch, timber and tiles or slates.
- Floors: trodden earth or clay, pebbles, stone slabs or tiles. Finishing: plaster, stone slabs, tiles, mosaics.

Use

- Occupation debris: (charcoal, ash, bone, organic debris) – on yard floors, less often in interiors.
- Hearths (burnt clay platforms).
- Repairs/modifications: blocked doors, raised floors.

Destruction/decay (NB roof falls before walls)

- Fire: charred timbers, reddened walls, fired-clay daub, shattered masonry.
- Earthquake: collapsed roofs, cracked or overturned masonry, floors out of horizontal alignment.
- Erosion: gradually by rain, wind, sea or burrowing animals; suddenly by landslide or flash floods.
- Robbing: as a quarry for building materials.
- Burial: by man for new buildings, by flooding, by natural deposition (wash levels), even volcanic action.

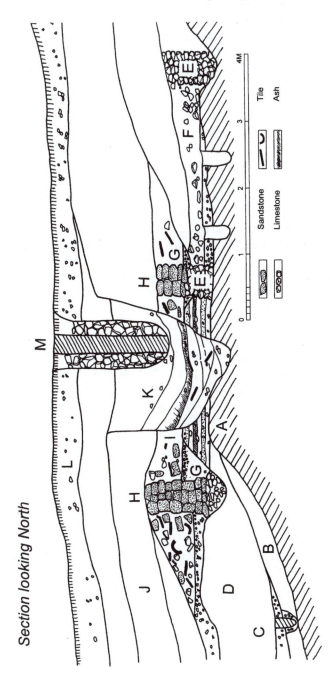

Section looking North

Fig 7.2 'Avonbury' - the imaginary section of a quarry face. Consider the strata and features shown and try to reconstruct the history of activity on the site. Compare your account with the explanation offered in Fig. 7.3.

Structures which are largely wooden will leave only shallow debris levels when they collapse and decay. Those made of mud-brick will leave much deeper levels but the bricks may only be detectable when still in position. Stone walls will often have been robbed. Roofs and upper structures may often only be reconstructed from fallen debris – broken tiles, lumps of clay baked in the destruction fires but bearing the impressions of timbers, etc. Only freak conditions such as the volcanic deposits at Pompeii and Thera preserve parts of the upper floor levels. Upper floors otherwise tend only to survive when buildings have been re-used continuously – such structures will have complex above-ground stratigraphy – or totally abandoned, whether because of war or dramatic decrease in agricultural prosperity, in remote areas (like parts of southern Turkey, northern Syria and north Africa) which have never been systematically re-occupied.

Many of the processes listed above result in the removal of evidence, wholly or partially. A section should always be read in terms of what is absent as well as what is present. Figure 7.1 illustrates a fairly straight-forward section at Çiftlik where more or less horizontal levels succeed each other. Study it carefully and then try to understand the more complicated diagram of an imaginary site 'Avonbury' (Fig. 7.2) in terms of the processes listed above. This illustrates the kind of sequence which might be encountered in a quarry face where no excavation has taken place to explain the features which have been cut through. Start by making a photocopy and marking on it the features you can identify. Then trace each stratigraphic division and see if you can work out the sequence of events. Perhaps it would help to use coloured pencils or markers to emphasise the levels as you identify them. Write out a history of the site and then compare it with the 'solution' offered on Figure 7.3. Often a number of different explanations may be equally possible.

Remember:

- Levels below are earlier – even if the angle of separation is very slight.

- Levels above are later

- Cuttings (pits, ditches etc) are later than the levels they cut through, however deep they go.

- Every building has a floor level, if not a laid floor, running between the walls.

7.2 Typology

The study of the objects found will normally continue in parallel with the study of the site itself. Each object will need to be classified according to material and, if known, function as the starting point of typological studies. Bronze objects for example, may be divided into tools, weapons, ornaments and scrap. Further functional subdivisions of ornaments might be pins, fibulae, bracelets, earrings and finger rings. The next stage is more difficult since different types of pins will reflect *fashion* rather than *function*. Grouping and classification at this level may well be subjective, if the objects are in a museum collection rather than from excavation, and can only be treated **typologically**.

Dating in this case is generally subjective, since there is no certainty about the order in which different types came into use or which were contemporary. It has been common in the past to assume that simple forms are early and complex forms are late as a type develops. In fact, simple and complex types may be contemporary and reflect only differences in market value and personal taste on the part of their purchasers. In the same way, items which require technical or artistic skill have often been classified according to the competence of their manufacture as good quality – earlier, or degenerate – later. There have, however, always been good and bad craftsmen, not to mention apprentices and experts.

In the context of an excavation, it should be possible to check the typological classifications against the stratigraphy. Earlier types should predominate in earlier levels: later types in later levels. Metalwork is, however, rare in settlement excavation: most was salvaged for recycling, and normally it is pottery typology which is most readily matched against the stratigraphic sequence as can be seen from the example below (Fig. 7.4).

7.3 The contribution of science

Few subjects are as genuinely multidisciplinary as archaeology, since virtually all the sciences from nuclear physics to genetic mapping can make their contribution to understanding the past, in just the same way as they can help to shape the future. It is the archaeologists' good fortune that a whole host of analytical techniques which have been developed for other purposes are available to enable new questions to be asked of the evidence they uncover. Although there is much truth in the old saying that a little knowledge is a dangerous thing, in the case of the field archaeologist a little knowledge of many subjects is highly desirable. There are many scientists with an interest in and enthusiasm for the

	Interpretation	*Finds Made*
A	Natural bedrock	
B	Deposit of brown soil	Hand-made pottery, Mesolithic flints
C	Post-pit cut into underlying soil containing small post and surrounded by pebbly layer forming floor surface, timber framed hut?	Hand-made pottery, coin of Julius Caesar, bronze fibula (brooch-like safety pin)
D	Fill of brown soil	Hand- and wheel-made pottery, Mesolithic flints
E	Walls of small rough stones on bedrock (W), in foundation trench (E). Pebble floor make-up between walls. Interior between walls, repeated levels of occupation debris in yard outside to W. Post-holes cut through floor for interior structure	Hand- and wheel-made pottery, mould-made red glazed 'Samian' pottery, coins of Caesar, Nero and Vespasian, iron nails: all from occupation levels
F	Debris level with rough stones from collapse of building	Wheel- and mould-made pottery, glass fragments, Mesolithic flints, coin of Augustus, lamps
G	Foundation trenches filled with small stones (W), and using old wall (E)	Hand-made pottery, glass, iron nail, coin of Hadrian
H	Stone walls of carefully chosen blocks. Floor level to E slightly higher than to W	
I	Fallen debris from collapse of building, tiles to W – therefore roofed, fewer stones to E, probably open area	Wheel-made pottery, Samian pottery, coins of Nero, Hadrian, Diocletian, roof tiles, glass fragments
J	Earth fill	Hand- and wheel-made pottery, coins of Augustus, Vespasian, Constantine the Great
K	Deep pit or ditch with successive layers of filling	Hand- and wheel-made pottery, brass belt clasp, coins of Claudius, Hadrian, Edward the Confessor
L	Surface soil with humus and roots	Samian pottery, willow pattern china, fragments of iron
M	Machine cut hole for telegraph/ electricity pole, packed with small stones	Hand- and wheel-made pottery, coin of Hadrian, sardine can

Fig 7.3 'Avonbury' – an interpretation and finds made.

ancient world who can provide fresh insights provided they are asked the *right* questions – and the right questions can only be asked if the archaeologist has sufficient knowledge of the processes involved and the kind of *samples* which may be required. We have already touched on the role of science in prospection (Chapter 4.4) and the study of plant and animal remains (Chapter 6.8) and will shortly look at its contribution to dating (Chapter 7.4). Other areas where science can play a part in the analysis of the finds can be roughly divided into composition and technology, trace elements and provenance, diet and health – though this list is far from exhaustive.

Chemical, spectrographic and **crystallographic analysis** can all be used to determine the component elements of pottery, metal and glass and to obtain clues about the temperature and methods of manufacture. It is important, for example, to determine whether the copper used for an artefact has been alloyed with tin (*tin-bronze*, used from the Early Bronze Age), lead (*lead bronze*, used from the Roman period) or zinc (*brass*, used from the mediaeval period). In the same way it is possible to understand some of the processes and skills of ancient technology which were needed for the casting of bronze statues, the manufacture of iron weapons, or the creation of elaborate *millefiori* glass (made of short rods fused side by side to create a pattern rather like Edinburgh rock).

With spectrography a sample of the material to be studied is burnt and each element present gives off light of a different wavelength of an intensity related to its quantity. Similar but even more accurate results can also be obtained by bombarding the material with atomic particles and examining the resultant patterns of absorption and reflection. These techniques reveal not only the principal components which give any material its physical characteristics but also *trace elements* which can act as 'fingerprints' that can sometimes be matched with the source of the raw materials and, by suggesting the provenance of the finished object, contribute to understanding the trade patterns of each period and region.

In pottery study these techniques can be used, for example, to determine the origin of the oil jars widely traded in the Mycenaean period, or of the Classical and Roman wine amphorae found in different parts of the Mediterranean. **Petrographic analysis** (the examination of thin sections of pottery under a powerful microscope) can also contribute to this kind of study by revealing the characteristic particles of different minerals in the fabric. In every provenance study the archaeologist has to provide a *control group* of examples of pottery whose origin is known for comparison with items which are thought to have originated in the same region but to have been traded long distances. The results of this kind of analysis, however, are often only probabilities, because while it is always possible to say no match has been found between the two sets of samples, a positive match is usually at the best tentative, pending the discovery of other possible places of origin.

Chemical techniques are less useful with bronze objects because the metal was so often re-melted as part of a mix of material of different origins. Here a different technique, **lead isotope analysis**, has had promising results. This depends on the existence of different isotopes of lead with different numbers of electrons. The proportions of each isotope present depend on the geological age of the metal ore and are unaffected by such physical processes as smelting or casting. Lead is naturally present in tiny quantities in most copper ores, as well as in all silver objects, so the method can be used for objects of all three metals. Greek coins, for example, can sometimes be traced to the mines which provided the metal.

Different techniques for determining organic trace elements (those which ultimately derive from living plants or animals) have been used with increasing success to determine the probable contents of pottery of different kinds. Compounds compatible with the compositions of olive oil, honey or wine have now regularly been identified in storage jars – though, as with pottery and metal, these results are no more than strong probabilities. Indeed when traces of two different substances such as wine and beer are found in the same jar it is not possible to say whether they were drunk *mixed* (perish the thought), or simply that the same jar had been used for both on different occasions. (It seems safe to assume that the standards of washing-up in the ancient world would not conform to modern health and safety regulations!)

Laboratory work on excavated bones can also produce exciting results. Extracted collagen can reveal the relative proportions of meat and fish in the diet; palaeopathology enables the study of ancient diseases by their effects on bone and teeth; DNA and trace elements can be extracted to provide evidence of where the person grew up; much work has been done in the field of facial reconstruction from skulls (most notably, perhaps, in the case of Philip II of Macedon).

Some deposits remain enigmatic even after they have been excavated and the sections studied. Scientific methods designed for understanding landscape change can sometimes help. The particle size of the soil may indicate whether its origin is natural or man-made, water-borne or wind-blown. Chemical analysis of phosphate traces can show whether it had a high organic content representing domestic refuse, agricultural processes (especially fertilising) or even burial. Similar analysis of wall plasters and other minerals such as slags from excavations may reveal something of the building materials or the industrial processes which took place in the vicinity. Most excavators take samples of the different deposits and unusual materials as the work progresses so that these are available if needed.

Finally, mention must be made of the mathematical and statistical techniques which enable the calculation of proportion and probability, or the quantification of coefficients of similarity, needed for the matching of pottery or metal compositions in the analytical techniques already described.

7.4 Dating

One of the first questions asked of any archaeological discovery – whether a single object or a complete site – is, naturally, 'what date is it?'. The answer can often be obtained only approximately. While a range of methods – historical, archaeological or scientific – are available, each has to be used with great caution. Even historical dates asserted with great confidence, such as the Greek colonisation of southern Italy or the foundation of Rome, rely on indirect evidence.

It is a rare object in the ancient world that carries on it a specific reference to the date of its creation, let alone any hint of the date when it was deposited where it was found. Exceptions include inscriptions of various kinds such as Athenian decrees that name the magistrates of the year, or Roman coins with the name of a Consul. All **absolute** systems of recording date, such as the use of the four-year Olympic cycle, rely on the existence of *written* historical sources which provide the framework within which the date can be determined. Special problems relate to dates in inscriptions which refer to city eras. These eras are based on traditional foundation dates, but cities sometimes started new eras when, for instance, their names were changed. The city of Soloi in Cilicia renamed itself as Pompeiopolis in 65 BC in honour of the Roman general Pompey and changed its dates from that point forward. Late Roman bricks made in Constantinople often have very legible stamped inscriptions carrying numbers in the indiction system. Unfortunately indictions were 15-year taxation periods and after each 15 years the numbering started again from the beginning. Since the form of the brickstamps varies, the indiction marks have been useful for securing a chronology in the typological sequence, even though their usefulness for providing absolute dates has been somewhat limited.

When dealing with purely **material** remains, whether in the prehistoric period or on the fringes of the Roman empire, the problem is more acute. While Greek historical sources provide a variety of dates for the Trojan War or for the 'Return of the Heraclidae' (descendants of Heracles), identifying these events in the archaeological record is fraught with difficulty – if indeed they *were* events in any modern sense. In dating Minoan and Mycenaean civilisation, references in Greek mythology have long been abandoned in favour of material cross-references to Egyptian civilisation.

Objects and contexts

When applying dates provided by any technique, careful thought has to be given to *what* is being dated. The *manufacture* of a gold scarab of Queen Nefertiti found in the Kaş shipwreck off southern Turkey or the *striking* of a coin of Hadrian found in the Roman fort at Housesteads on Hadrian's Wall can both be dated within a few years. The date at which the boat sank or the auxiliary soldier dropped his pay in a latrine must be later but *how much later* remains in question. The relationship between the object and the context in which it was found must also be considered carefully. The scarab, for example, provides a *terminus post quem* (date after which) for the sinking of the Kaş wreck but the coin tells us only that the latrine was *in use* after the coin was struck, not when it was *constructed*. Similarly, an event can provide a *terminus ante quem* (date before which) for a group of objects associated with it. At Masada in Israel, life in the fortress ceased with its sack by the Romans in AD 73, so we can be confident that the objects of pottery, iron and other materials found were in use before then, but we do not know how much earlier they were manufactured. Confidence is often misplaced unless supported by other evidence: does a burnt level at Troy reflect its sack by the Homeric heroes? Is the thick black layer of burnt material at Colchester really the work of Boudicca's rampaging warriors?

Fortunately the archaeologist rarely has to rely on a single source of information to establish the date of a discovery. The general chronological framework already established and the combination of a variety of objects all help to narrow down the period in which an event may have occurred or an item was deposited. On a site like Housesteads a range of different Roman coins can be found in any one stratum. The *latest* of these coins gives the *earliest* date for the creation of the stratum in question. It is also likely that coins of any given issue will gradually disappear from circulation so that the presence of several of similar date suggests the *probability* that they were issued not long before.

Once the dates of particular classes of pottery have been established they can be used to date new contexts. The latest pottery gives the earliest date for a level. The majority however may be misleading. Pottery is almost indestructible; once broken it becomes of no more interest (except to the archaeologist) than the pebbles which accompany it. In archaeological terms it has become **residual**. A single Roman sherd in a defensive ditch cut through an Iron Age settlement will give the earliest date for the ditch though found with many sherds hundreds of years older. At Mycenae walls of mud-brick incorporate dozens of much older sherds mixed with the clay of which they are built. When these walls collapse, it takes a sharp eye to spot the few distinctive pieces which may date the construction or use of the building. It is equally important to make sure that levels have not been contaminated by pits or animal burrows. Modern coins can mysteriously find their way into Roman levels and their presence must be explained.

To recap, contexts may be dated *in relative terms* from the objects found in them and, in turn, objects or materials may be dated by the contexts in which they are found. Statements such as 'built before' or 'used later than' can often be made with confidence, but statements such as 'dates to the thirteenth century BC' or 'used in the reign of Hadrian' are usually no more than *probabilities* supported by a range of evidence. Individual items, especially those divorced from their context, will rarely be datable, but groups of objects from a single context may well provide a firm date for that context.

When you have checked the 'solution' in Fig. 7.3 against your own history of Avonbury, it is time to work out the date of each deposit using the information given there. Answers can be found on page 138.

Relative chronology

Relative chronologies have little to do with exact periods of time, but more with sequences of material built up on a local scale and then matched with sequences adjacent in both time and space (Fig. 7.4). If these are to be reliable they must depend on stratigraphy. Simple principles to be observed in establishing sequences of material include:

- each level is dated by the latest item in it;
- the first appearance of any item is far more significant than its continued use;
- *residual* objects are normal not exceptional;
- no safe assessment can be made of the lifespan of a single item.

Correlations can be established between two areas with different material cultures which exchange goods through trade or other means, but their

Mycenaean pottery is very varied in shape and decoration. The shapes shown are a few of those typical of late (top) or early (bottom) levels. Complete vessels are used here though in practice only sherds from them would be found. In constructing a typology it is the *first appearance* of each type which is significant, though some types may continue in use and early sherds are frequently found in later levels.

Fig 7.4 A schematic diagram to illustrate the principles of constructing the relative chronology of Mycenaean pottery. Three sites (A-C) provide stratified sequences of pottery which can be correlated by comparing the first appearance and maximum popularity of specific shapes at each site. Use the information provided to draw up a list of the different types in the order of their first appearance.

NB each section of the table represents a distinct level but no information is available to indicate what period of time each represents.

accuracy depends on the quantity of goods exchanged, their durability and whether the process of exchange is bi-directional. This form of correlation has been used to link sequences in Bronze-Age Greece with those of Egypt. Minoan and Mycenaean pottery vessels were regularly exported to Syria and Egypt for their contents but kept in use for only a short period, while scarabs of different Egyptian Pharaohs were regarded as items of jewellery or talismans. As such they often remained in circulation for many years. Unfortunately, the total quantities are small and many Egyptian finds are from old excavations where the stratigraphic evidence was not accurately recorded. Although a chronological framework has been constructed with great care, there are many weak links and new evidence from *scientific* methods has already challenged the validity of the framework.

Once a sequence has been established, dates within it must be obtained in relation to some other point of reference, which in turn may depend on one further removed. Although the sequence of events or fashions in pottery or other material may be clear, with each stage the margin of error increases so that the dates become steadily less definite. Relative chronology is rather like an elastic band which can be stretched at any part of its length to increase one time interval or to decrease another. Although many attempts have been made to determine the length of a period from the quantity of material belonging to it, or to assess the duration of a period of occupation from the depth of the deposits which accumulated, both are fallacious. Only cross-references to **absolute chronologies** can help fix part of the sequence in time, to fasten down as it were, particular parts of the elastic band.

Absolute chronology

Until the 1950s the only 'absolute' cross-references were to historical dates, often themselves subject to discussion. The Greek 'Dark Ages', for example, were dated with reference to only two 'fixed' points. Pottery of derivative Mycenaean type was found in Syria in a destruction level attributed to the campaigns of Rameses III, dated to 1193 BC on the authority of written sources. This pottery marked, in mainland Greece, the first levels after the destruction of the Palaces at Mycenae and Pylos. For another four-and-a-half centuries there is nothing firm to which to fasten the elastic band of relative chronology until the appearance of Greek colonies in Southern Italy with Middle and Late Geometric pottery imported from Corinth. According to Herodotus and other ancient historians many of these colonies were *formally* founded in the second half of the seventh century BC when the mother city sent out an official party of colonists. All dates between these points are still purely 'conventional', used for lack of anything better.

Even these fixed points can be questioned. Are we sure the destruction levels at Megiddo are the work of Rameses III rather than some accidental fire? Does the Corinthian pottery date to the earliest levels of the *formal* colony? The elastic band is in serious danger of snapping back in our faces.

Science has now, however, come to the aid of the archaeologist with a range of methods which are capable of providing dates independent of the archaeological material or the relative chronology. Carbon 14 (C^{14}) dating has been regularly in use since 1960, though it has been most helpful when applied in earlier prehistory where the combination of relative and historical chronology is impossible. Dendrochronology has been applied since about 1980 to later historical periods and is rapidly becoming more useful even as far back as the Mycenaean period. Other techniques can make a valuable contribution in certain circumstances. It is not our purpose to explain in detail the scientific basis of these techniques, which is set out in many reference books, but to explain the principles underlying the two most useful, C^{14} and dendrochronology, and their applicability.

Carbon 14 Dating

Most plants take in Carbon dioxide (CO_2) during photosynthesis and incorporate the carbon into their cell structure. Most of this carbon is the standard isotope C^{13} but a small proportion is the unstable isotope C^{14} with one additional electron, created in the earth's upper atmosphere by solar radiation. The release of the extra electron as this isotope decays can be detected either passively, or by *acceleration* techniques (using nuclear energy to speed up the decay process). It has been known since 1950 that the half-life (the period during which half of the remaining C^{14} is transformed into C^{13}) is 5730 ± 40 years. Any surviving carbon of plant origin can therefore theoretically be dated within a defined margin of experimental and statistical error. The archaeological applications of this technique were rapidly appreciated, especially for distant prehistoric periods for which chronology at best depended on an educated estimate. Although uncharred wood rapidly decays except in unusually arid conditions such as are found in Egypt, charred wood (charcoal) is virtually indestructible except by mechanical means.

Typically, charred wood from building timbers has been chosen as the subject of C^{14} determinations. The resulting date relates to the moment at which incorporation of the carbon ceased. In the case of a tree this is the point at which a new 'living' ring enclosed the year-old one inside it. Thus unless the bark is still present on the sample (which rarely occurs), the date is not that of felling but some years earlier when the last ring in the sample was laid down.

Since herbivores consume large quantities of vegetation they, too, incorporate carbon into their bodies and bones, while carnivores continue the food chain and thus transmission of the rare isotope. Both human and animal bones can be the subject of C^{14} determinations, though usually these need the expensive acceleration techniques to achieve them. In this case the *death* of the animal is the reference point.

C^{14} determinations are usually cited by the laboratories which have carried them out in terms such as 3050 ±50 bp, or 1650 ±20 bp where the ± indicates the statistical error based on 70% probability. The term 'bp' (abbreviation for 'before present') refers to the date to which all calculations are referred by the laboratories, with 'present' having been set at AD 1950 rather than to the present day. Most archaeological publications convert these dates to BC or AD figures to help the reader, but recently calibration has been applied to make the dates more precise and to allow for fluctuations in the atmospheric pool of C^{14}. This however is only helpful in earlier prehistoric periods since it remains true that historically based dates in the archaeology of the Classical world are very often more accurate than those supplied by C^{14} techniques, with their relatively wide margins of statistical error.

Dendrochronology

It has long been known that trees add a ring to their girth annually and that the age of a tree can be determined simply by counting rings. It has also been recognised that these rings provided a record of climatic conditions where the tree was growing, since drought or exceptional cold resulted in a underdeveloped ring, while an unusually long or favourable growing season would result in a thick one. Only with the application of computer-matching techniques was it possible to make comparisons of trees or pieces of timber on a large enough scale to discover that the patterns of growth over 20-30 years were unique to that period for any given area. In many cases major climatic events could be traced from one area to another, while overlapping patterns in different samples have allowed a composite sequence to be constructed covering hundreds of years (Fig. 7.5). Although the study of dendrochronology started with climatic history as its principal goal, as the database of material built up it rapidly became obvious that its potential for dating material from archaeological contexts in both Europe and the Near East was immense.

Whilst the potential of the technique is enormous as accurate reference sequences are gradually built up, surviving ancient timbers with as many as the 50 rings necessary for matching, or the 100 necessary to extend the sequence significantly, are rare. There is the further consideration that unless the bark is present, the outermost surviving ring in a piece

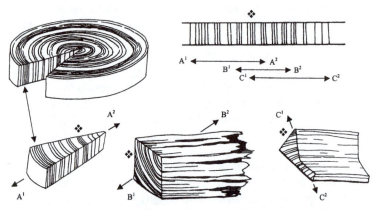

Fig 7.5 Constructing a dendrochronology sequence. Every tree records in its growth rings the climatic pattern of successive years: thick rings indicate wetter or warmer conditions, thin rings colder or dryer conditions. In the simplified diagram above each piece of timber shares (most obviously) a group of four closely spaced growth rings marked ❖.

of timber was determined by the carpenter who may have sawn or trimmed many rings away. A continuous sequence exists from the present back to the Roman period and a timber from a seventh-century BC tomb at Gordion in western Anatolia must reach back to the Bronze Age. Valuable results have been obtained for mediaeval churches in Greece and Turkey, where the date of building materials often matches with, but also sometimes contradicts, the dedicatory inscriptions.

On a global scale, climatic episodes have been identified which seem to coincide with historical events such as the end of the Mycenaean World or the migrations in the late Roman period. Whether these are purely coincidental or whether climatic change had some dramatic impact on the course of civilisation is still a matter of hot debate. Indeed some scholars see these episodes as the result of devastating meteorite impact on the earth's surface.

Proceed with caution!

It is impossible to read (or write) the account of any period or topic in relation to the Classical world without reference to dates. To omit these would be to remove the landmarks which chart the progress of developments in material culture and in the society they reflect. Make sure that you, the reader, understand the system used. Archaeologists write with reference to periods of material culture (the Shaft Grave Period) or to sequences of pottery (Late Helladic IIIB, Late Geometric) so that their account is still accurate even if the date of the culture or of the pottery changes. Historians tend to write with reference to fixed periods (the reign of Nero) or dates (the fourth century AD) in the expectation that these will not need to be changed.

Even when the dates are clear, historical and archaeological data can tell different stories as in the case of the richly furnished tomb at Vergina (ancient Aegae) in Macedonia, which is usually thought of as that of Philip II. This grave has no inscription to identify either the man or the woman whose partially cremated remains were contained in two gold chests. On the façade is a painting showing Philip and Alexander hunting. The grave goods include a gold circlet with the knot of Herakles which symbolised kingship in ancient Macedon. The skull of a mature male from the chest in the inner chamber shows the kind of injury to the right eye socket sustained in life by Philip outside the walls of Methone. The inference that this is indeed Philip's tomb, hastily finished after his murder in the theatre at Aegae in 332 BC, is hard to escape. Some of the minor pottery objects of Athenian manufacture, however, do not occur in Athens until 30 years later, and their presence has given rise to speculation that this is another member of the Macedonian Royal House or that the burial was completely refurnished at some later date. No easy solution is yet available to explain the discrepancies and we do not know whether, eventually, the Athenian pottery will be redated or the identification with Philip will have to be abandoned.

7.5 Interpretation

At every stage of the archaeologist's work there is some degree of interpretation, of subjective judgement based on the evidence available. This ranges from the simplest identification of objects to deciding whether a building is public or private, or to reconstructing the nature of cult activity from the objects found. Sometimes the process is almost unconscious – for example, a metal object with a cutting edge and handle is usually defined as a knife. At other times reference is required to ancient written sources, or to modern accounts of more 'primitive' technologies or societies, to try and identify objects which are not immediately comprehensible. In such cases the parallels can only suggest possibilities, because usually they will be drawn from other parts of the world and other periods. In extreme cases no contemporary parallel is forthcoming, and the object or structure has to be interpreted provisionally. A good example of this sort of problem is the structure interpreted as a *gyrus* (horse-training ring) in the Lunt Roman fort in Warwickshire. What was found was a large circular enclosure which *could* have been used for breaking in horses or training cavalrymen in the way which is described by the *Greek* historian Xenophon. Xenophon was writing 400 years before the Lunt was constructed, so the identification is somewhat tentative.

Very often the context in which an object is found may help to identify it or its function. Thus the fact that the Lunt was a cavalry fort strengthens the supposition that the circular structure was a *gyrus*. The pieces of jewellery found on either side of the skull in a burial are likely to be earrings, while pins found at shoulder level probably held clothing in position. A double row of conical clay objects with suspension holes may be identified as weights from a vertical loom. Ancient oil presses can be recognised by comparison with their modern counterparts. Some objects were used in different ways in different contexts. Bowls may be used for feasting, for offerings in sanctuaries or in the Christian church for baptism, for decoration, even built into the walls. Amphorae may be used as containers for oil or wine, for use in building vaults or domes to reduce the weight or under floors as a form of damp-proofing. Broken-off bases of amphorae turn up as urinals in Roman forts.

The function of buildings and the rooms in them may be deduced from the finds – though in the case of Greek and Roman buildings the detailed descriptions of Vitruvius can often be illuminating. Large clay jars imply storage areas, though the commodity stored – grain, oil or wine – may not be immediately obvious. Hearths may indicate cooking areas when found with the typical cooking wares, but elsewhere may represent workshops or industrial activities. Expensive materials such as marble or elaborate decoration, including wall-paintings, may be used for the most important buildings in a town or the most important room in a house but will not necessarily show whether these are public or private. Inscriptions may indicate whether the building has a sacred or, occasionally, another function, as at Ostia in the case of the shipping exchange.

With the exception of such obvious cases as Greek temples where a specific architectural form became standard, the identification of sacred places is often fraught with difficulty. In the case of the great archaic sanctuaries known from historical sources, excavation has revealed assemblages of distinctive objects associated with each: offerings of weapons and jewellery, tripod cauldrons and figurines of various types. Smaller sanctuaries can be recognised from the presence of similar objects, as in the case of the cave at Polis on the island of Ithaka which was clearly associated in antiquity with the return of Odysseus. In later periods fired clay (terracotta) figurines are often found in quantity in sacred places but may also be found in tombs, or in the workshops where they were made. At the Macedonian capital, Pella, a figurine workshop was recognised from the presence of the moulds in which the figurines had been cast as well as the figurines themselves.

In the Bronze Age the problem is even more acute. The 'Temple' at Mycenae contained a unique series of large clay figures and clay snakes, together with quantities of ordinary domestic pottery and other familiar objects. One of the figures was found standing on the unusual benches in the main room. A central platform may have served as a sacred hearth. Taken as a whole, the assemblage of finds is so unusual that a sacred function seems likely for this building. Individually, none of the features provides a compelling argument. It is unlikely that the small figurines found everywhere in Mycenaean Greece of themselves mark religious activity, even though some 'domestic' shrines equivalent to the Lares and Penates of Roman tradition may well have existed.

Consider the following assemblage, which we might, as archaeologists, completely misinterpret. Investigation of a building ruined by fire reveals a built hearth set against a wall, piled high with ashes. Nearby are found a large bronze cauldron and a knobbed sceptre. Smashed among the ashes are highly decorated vessels of glass and pottery in unusual forms. There are two shattered clay figurines, one male and one female. The latter is of a different, perhaps earlier style, and may have been treasured for many years. There are twisted and corroded pieces of metal of different kinds. This was clearly a sacred place, with a fire burning, figures for veneration, valuable vessels for offerings to placate the gods and ceremonial equipment.

What is the date of this assemblage? It belongs to the mid-twentieth century. The finds indicate not a prehistoric sanctuary but a modern British fireplace with coal scuttle and poker, and ornaments on the mantelpiece including grandma's favourite Meissen shepherd and shepherdess. The metallic remains are those of a clock or perhaps a television set. The only rituals observed here were those of afternoon tea or watching Eastenders, though some would say these were equal in social and cultural significance to the obscure rituals of the Aegean Bronze Age.

7.6 Publication

Unless publication follows, any research is a waste of time and effort. Unreported finds in museum store-rooms might as well still be buried on site. Obviously it is not possible to report every detail, and much should be left as archival material accessible for later study.

The usual pattern for the academic presentations of results is for each season to be reported in lectures or in print with the short *preliminary* conclusions. *Final* publication when study is complete is usually much more substantial. A typical report, which may run to several volumes depending on the scale of the project, whether survey or excavation, will contain a wide range of studies by different specialists. In the case of an excavation, these studies will typically include stratigraphy and architecture, accounts of the different classes of finds (pottery, metal, stone etc.) together with discussions of their relationship to other known material. Scientific specialists are likely to contribute sections on the general environment, the plant and animal remains, or technical studies of pottery or metals. Overviews of the nature of the site and of the activities carried out there, as well as of its significance in a broader context, are essential, and may well form the basis of the accounts aimed at a wider audience.

Every report should be a work of reference with clear photographs, drawings, diagrams or graphs as appropriate. Cross-indexing is essential since few reports are read continuously from beginning to end but are more often dipped into for different classes of information. Many archaeologists start with the illustrations as the quickest way to understand the discoveries at any site, especially in dealing with the Classical world where publication may be in any one of a large number of languages. Archaeology is one of the few sciences where English has not become the standard language.

Traditionally publication has been with print on paper but new technologies are constantly increasing the possibilities for presenting the results of archaeological research. Microfilm or microfiche are cheap but not very convenient ways of publishing quantities of data in support of the printed text. CD-Rom is rapidly being developed as a way of producing similar data in an interactive form cheaply, while the Internet is being used in the same way, especially for the more succinct popular accounts. These new techniques allow the unrestricted use of colour images and rapid searches for relevant information. Video documentaries are also particularly vivid ways of presenting information for educational purposes.

Like all specialists, however, the archaeologist has to take particular care to present popular reports in an accessible manner without jargon or obscure references. While an interest in the past is perhaps more general now than ever before, it is still important that this interest continues to be fostered by archaeologists themselves. The days of scholarship in 'Ivory Towers' are fortunately long past in most disciplines.

7.7 Presentation and display of archaeological sites

The director of an excavation may also have to devote thought and resources to presenting the site to the public as a monument. If the excavation was conducted for rescue purposes, there may be no obligation to ensure the survival and accessibility, let alone display, of the site. Where, however, an important site has been uncovered for research purposes – or, indeed, a rescue excavation has revealed something so important that the proposed development which prompted the excavation has had to be abandoned or altered in order to accommodate display of structures – the archaeological project may have extended into a further final stage concerned with consolidation and display of archaeological features, and fund-raising to provide a purpose-built site museum or visitor centre.

Displaying an archaeological site is a complicated business. There are difficult ethical questions to answer about whether to reveal what was excavated just as it was excavated, or whether to engage in partial reconstruction in order to help public understanding and improve the site's value as an educational resource. Where remains are consolidated for display this must be done sympathetically with appropriate materials which follow the basic principle of conservation that nothing should be added which is stronger than the original materials, or which will react chemically with them. Consolidated areas of a monument must also be visibly different, if only very slightly, so that there can be no confusion in the future about which features are original to the site. Any building work which is necessary must be documented and recorded as carefully as the excavation process which preceded it.

The ultimate decision about how to display may relate to the nature of the materials revealed – it is harder to display the traces of burnt timber buildings than of stone structures – or to the conclusions which emerge from analysis of the results of excavation, since a choice may have to be made between displaying one period of a multi-period site or trying to show elements from all periods. This issue may also affect the excavation if features have to be preserved for the sake of display even though they overlie earlier ones. Often it is appropriate to attempt reconstructions. These can be at reduced scale (models or computer graphics) or full-scale buildings erected over or near the original foundations. When the decision is taken to reconstruct, this can involve the archaeologist in another stage of research into the sources of ancient building materials, the recipes for ancient mortars, or the methods of working with timber. Often this leads to exercises in **experimental archaeology** which increase our understanding about, say, the methods of prefabrication and the durability of ancient timber structures (as at the Lunt Roman Fort), or the practicality of suggested interpretations for puzzling features. Such exercises commonly increase modern respect for ancient craftmanship, as it becomes clear that it is can be extraordinarily difficult and expensive to reproduce objects found in excavations of Classical sites.

Public access inevitably results in increased wear and tear on any site. The decision to present a site for display can only be justified where it will not lead to an unacceptable degree of deterioration of the physical remains. It can only proceed if the resources are available both for consolidating and displaying the monument, and for maintaining the site for the foreseeable future. The ability to sustain the display long after excavation and research are completed is of paramount importance. In many cases the archaeologist responsible may ultimately conclude that the best interests of an excavated monument may well be served by reburying the remains. This too must be done with great care so that the buried remains do not deteriorate further. A permeable membrane is first laid to separate the structures from the back fill – often the spoil which was removed from around them – while allowing the natural drainage of the site to continue as it had for many centuries before excavation. Not only will the site be well protected in this way but the landscape will be returned as nearly as possible to the condition in which the archaeologist found it.

The methods of archaeology may have changed in the past hundred years but the words of Sir Leonard Woolley in *Dead Towns and Living Men*, largely written in a Turkish prisoner of war camp between 1916 and 1918, still describe the work of the archaeologist, more succinctly than we have and perhaps more resonantly:

> There *is* a romance in digging, but for all that it is a trade wherein long periods of steady work are only occasionally broken by a sensational discovery and even then the success of the season depends, as a rule, not on the rare 'find' that loomed so large for the moment, but on the information drawn with time and patience out of the mass of petty detail which the day's routine little by little brought to light and set in due perspective.

How to become an archaeologist

This book is about *methods* and the best way to understand methods is naturally to put them into practice. However keen you are on archaeology we don't expect you will have the chance to direct your own project just yet, but there are many ways in which you can begin to learn and understand and there are often opportunities to participate in projects in the UK. Once you have some experience you may be able to help with a project elsewhere in the Classical world.

Some of you, of course, are looking forward to, or have just begun, a university degree course including a substantial element of practical archaeological work in the field or in the laboratory; and this must be the best way to pursue and develop an ambition for an archaeological career, or to obtain skills which will enable you to participate in projects as a volunteer even if your career lies in a different direction.

Many of you, however, have not yet reached this stage and may well be wondering how to become involved and perhaps improve your chances of gaining a place at university to read for a degree including archaeology. Others, perhaps, have passed the stage of a degree but want to get involved in the discovery of the past in a practical way on an 'amateur' basis. So, what next?

Join your local archaeological or historical society. Look out for lecture courses offered in your area by local universities or other organisations. Visit archaeological sites, and 'digs' in progress. Ask sensible questions – we all like to talk about our work, but choose your moment! Volunteer to help, but be committed. It takes time to train newcomers. Visit museums and collections: be critical and ask yourself, not 'what is it?' but 'what do we learn from this?' Watch the television programmes: What have they left out? The routine work is not often good television.

Visit the Web and look for reports on sites you can use as case studies to improve your understanding of the methods and goals of archaeological research. We have tried to provide a starting point but things change fast and new discoveries are posted all the time. Look for the project site or a university teaching site rather than the this-is-where-I-went-on-my-holidays kind of page. Try and answer the following questions as we have explored them in the previous pages:

- What problems did the excavation address?
- How was the project planned and organised?
- What preliminary prospection was necessary?
- What strategy of excavation or survey was employed?
- What finds were made and did they require special treatment?
- What date is the site and what activities took place there?
- How is publication being organised and what is on display?

You can try some things out for yourself, and we have already provided a small number of exercises. Look at aerial photographs of sites and work out what you can see. Plan how you would start to investigate each with an excavation. Borrow tape measures and string and plan the room you work in or your garden and its pathways. Make a water level and try it out – it may even come in handy in levelling the new pond for the garden or other non-archaeological activities. If you have a camera, take careful photographs of a site near you – but *not* one where an excavation is taking place without asking permission since you might make yourself very unwelcome. Do your photographs show clearly what you intended? Mount them in the centre of a large piece of paper and annotate all the features with what they are. Look at the stratigraphic diagrams in this book and see if you can 'read' them.

Remember that archaeology borrows skills from many other disciplines and if you have any of these you may well become a valuable member of a project team. There is always work for good photographers, illustrators and surveyors. Scientists may well have expertise to offer – or may be able to adapt existing techniques to archaeological problems. Many of the scientific methods we have described in this book were developed 'on the side'. There is always work for the computer literate in creating interactive catalogues, preparing reports, publications or web sites. If you understand mathematical and statistical procedures your assistance will be welcome in preparing numerical analyses of finds. Projects abroad may well need the help of a book-keeper or a house-keeper to make sure everything runs smoothly. Here knowledge of the local language is an enormous advantage – few projects take place in the kind of tourist area where everyone speaks English more fluently than we do!

Suggestions for Further Reading

General

L. Adkins, and R.A. Adkins, *A Thesaurus of British Archaeology* (London, David & Charles, 1982).

P. Bahn, *Bluff Your Way in Archaeology* (London, Ravette, 1989).

W. Bray and D. Trump, *A Dictionary of Archaeology* (London, Penguin, 1970).

B.M. Fagan, *In the Beginning: an Introduction to Archaeology* (New York, HarperCollins, 1991.

C. Gamble, *Archaeology, the Basics* (London, Routledge, 2001).

K. Greene, *Archaeology an Introduction* (3rd ed., London, Routledge, 1996).

P. Halkon, *An Archaeological Resource Book for Teachers* (York; Council for British Archaeology, 1992).

C. Renfrew and P. Bahn, *Archaeology; Theories, Methods and Practice* (2nd ed., London, Thames and Hudson, 1996).

T. Taylor, C. Lewis, P. Harding, M. Aston, *Time Team's Timeschester, a Companion to Archaeology* (Channel 4 Books, 2000).

R.D. Whitehouse, *The Macmillan Dictionary of Archaeology* (Basingstoke, Macmillan, 1983).

The Development of Archaeology

G. Daniel, *A Short History of Archaeology* (London, Thames and Hudson, 1981).

B.G. Trigger, *A History of Archaeological Thought* (Cambridge, CUP, 1989).

M. Vickers, *The Roman World* (Chap. 2, Oxford, Elsevier-Phaidon, 1977).

R. Weiss, *The Renaissance Discovery of Classical Antiquity* (Oxford, Blackwells, 1969, 1988).

Methods and Techniques

M.J. Aitken, *Science-based dating in Archaeology* (London, Longman, 1990).

G. Andrews, *Management of Archaeological Projects* (London, English Heritage, 1991).

M. Aston, *Interpreting the Landscape* (London, Batsford, 1992).

P. Barker, *Techniques of Archaeological Excavation* (3rd ed., London, Batsford, 1993).

A. Brown, *Fieldwork for Archaeologists and Local Historians* (London, Batsford, 1987).

M. Carver, *Underneath English Towns: Interpreting Urban Archaeology* (London, Batsford, 1987).

A. Clark, *Seeing Beneath the Soil* (London, Batsford, 1991).

T. Darvill, *Ancient Monuments in the Countryside* (London, English Heritage, 1987).

S.J.M. Davis, *The Archaeology of Animals* (London, Batsford, 1987).

P.L. Drewett, *Field Archaeology an Introduction* (London, UCL, 1999).

S. McCready, *Archaeological Field Survey in Britain and Abroad* (London, Society of Antiquaries, 1985).

J. McIntosh, *The Practical Archaeologist* (London, Thames and Hudson, 1999).

K. Muckelroy, *Maritime Archaeology* (Cambridge, CUP, 1978).

R. Payton, *Retrieval of Objects from Archaeological Sites* (Denbigh, Archetype Publications, 1992).

C. Spence (ed.), *Archaeological Site Manual* (London, Museum of London, 1990).

D. Watkinson (ed.), *First Aid for Finds* (2nd ed., London, Rescue, 1987).

D.R. Wilson, *Air Photo Interpretation for Archaeologists* (London, Batsford, 1982).

Shire Series (Shire Publications, Princes Risborough: * = in print)

R.W. Bagshawe, *Roman Roads* (10, 1979, 1994)*.

P.J. Casey, *Roman Coinage in Britain* (12, 1980, 1984, 1994)*.

G. de la Bédoyère, *Pottery in Roman Britain* (79, 2000)*.

J. Dyer, *Teaching Archaeology in Schools* (29, 1983).

R. Hanley, *Villages in Roman Britain* (49, 2000)*.

G. Lock & J. Wilcock, *Computer Archaeology* (51, 1987).

R.M. Luff, *Animal Remains in Archaeology* (33, 1984).

D.N. Riley, *Aerial Archaeology in Britain* (22, 1996).

A. Stirland, *Human Bones in Archaeology* (46, 1986, 1999)*.

M. Taylor, *Wood in Archaeology* (17, 1981)*.

J.P. Wild, *Textiles in Archaeology* (56, 1988)*.

Case Studies

J.G. Evans, *Land and Archaeology* (London, Tempus, 1999).

B.M. Fagan, *Eyewitness to Discovery* (London, Batsford, 1992).

M. Grant, *The Visible Past: Greek and Roman History from Archaeology 1960-1990* (London, Weidenfeld and Nicolson, 1990).

I. Morris, *Classical Greece: Ancient Histories and Modern Archaeologies* (Cambridge, CUP, 1994).

T. Taylor, *The Ultimate Time Team Companion* (Basingstoke, Macmillan, 1999).

C. Vita-Finzi, *Archaeological Sites in their Setting* (Basingstoke, Thames & Hudson, 1978).

Index

Solution to Avonbury dating exercise Fig. 7.3
B: Pre Roman; C: Pre Roman, after 56 BC; D: ? Roman influenced: after 56 BC; EE: Roman, after AD 69; F: Roman, after AD 69; GG: Roman, after AD 117; I: Roman, after AD 284; J: Roman, after AD 312; K: Saxon/Norman, after AD 1042; L: Modern, after AD 1750; M: Modern, after AD 1850.